CAPTAIN NIBLICK
The World's Worst Golf Skipper

Cover artwork devised by John Michael Wade and executed by
David Green
and John Maclean

Rev. date: 01/07/2014

To order additional copies of this book, contact:
Xlibris LLC
0800-056-3182
www.xlibrispublishing.co.uk
Orders@Xlibrispublishing.co.uk

Also by John Michael Wade

Valet's Diction - *an Edwardian odyssey and its distant echoes*

The book tells the tale of an English manservant travelling to a fishing lodge in Norway in 1906 and the subsequent return journey by the grandson he never knew. Published by Gaffer Press, London, it is available from the author at 7 Carlina Gardens, IG8 0BP, UK, at a cost of £5 including post and packing. Send a cheque made out to the author to the above address for fast despatch.

* Also visit *www.superart.info* for video versions of the Outlaw Sketch, listed under Performance Art, and other artworks.

CAPTAIN NIBLICK

JOHN MICHAEL WADE

INTRODUCTION

The captain of a golf club is a figurehead, the public face of the assorted membership. He is a leader of men (and women), a speech-maker, a promoter of his club, a man with deep pockets and, invariably a half-decent golfer.

But what does he actually do? What are the problems he faces? How does he overcome them? And what, in essence, is his role—stooge or activist?

To answer these questions, I was given unprecedented access to the life and times of one such skipper, a certain Mashie Niblick, a former caddy, when he became the newly-minted Captain of a small club buried beneath a multitude of trees in one of the great forests of England. It is a rum tale.

Indeed, it is a remarkable story of continuity, of change, of slapstick humour, and of deadly seriousness. Over the course of the year 2013, it changed Niblick irrevocably. He had never ever spent as much time on the fairways in his 60-year golfing life. He went from worse to dire in his play to end up, as he freely admitted, to be the world's worst golfing skipper.

As his amanuensis, I have charted his progress—or rather regress—from the time he stepped up to the plate to the time he stepped down from his role. I have admired him from afar and closely in his pits when drink has got the better of him.

This is the true record of a hero, a somewhat tarnished hero in truth, but a hero nevertheless. I am proud to tell the story of his amazing life as a captain.

JOHN MICHAEL WADE

Disguised as Robin Hood, Captain Niblick gallops across the greensward

CONTENTS

Hole 1: The Dell

Hole 2: Leeward

Hole 3: Mornington

Hole 4: Woodside

Hole 5: The Whinns

Hole 6: Brambles

Hole 7: Punch Bowl

Hole 8: Gravel Pits

Hole 9: Sunset

Hole 10: Pilgrims

Hole 11: Stylish

Hole 12: Erectile dysfunction

Hole 13: Goody no shoes

Hole 14: Port

Hole 15: Slagheaps

Hole 16: Bunnymen

Hole 17: Heroic failure

Hole 18: Curtain down

Hole 19: Imposter

Captain Niblick first published 2014

"I regard golf as an expensive way of playing marbles"

- G K Chesterton (1874-1936)

Riding his hobby horse Woody and blowing his hunting horn, Robin Hood (Niblick) is pursued by Alan A'Dale (Terry Insole) with his ukulele

A hole in one is golfing nirvana whether it be a brilliant shot or a fluke. The outcome is perfection. It lifts a player into the realms of the gods. Momentarily, he inhabits Heaven.

At the other end of this sporting spectrum, there was Mashie Niblick, a barfly whose golfing prowess—or rather lack of it—placed him in the realm of Hades. He roundly acknowledged his incompetence to his barfly mates, eventually rating himself the world's worst golfing captain.

It came about like this. The 2012 club captain was at his wits' end with all the safe members turning down his invitation to become his vice-captain and subsequently the 2013 captain. In utter desperation late on in the year, he turned to Mashie Niblick, the last man standing. Now Mashie had once served on the club's management committee but quit as the club's press officer after an altercation with prominent members over some trivial issue. He thought the likelihood of his ever becoming a leader of golfers was as remote as him winning more than £25 on the handful of Premium Bonds he held.

After all, he took up the game after a spell as a caddy and then lost golf balls around the world for 60 years. Mashie Niblick rated himself one of the dodgiest players in the club whose wild zig-zag play had once lost him 12 balls over 18 holes, surely a British record. And this cheery chappie had just finished 20th out of 20 pals golfing on the sunny Costa del Sol and yet he reckoned that he was the luckiest bugger alive because his mates forgot to bring out the "thong of shame" which normally tail-end-Charlie has to don for a naked dash down the Torremolinos sands to the sea and back to the derision of beach babes.

Mashie Niblick was puzzled. He posed some questions that had no sensible answers. What me, with an official handicap of 26 and a severe inability to chip and putt apart from on those immensely bumpy greens on the cliff-top Castle course at St Andrews? What me, at 74, a balding veteran who recalled being given a set of wooden clubs by an uncle—a former club captain—who wanted to encourage me to take up the game? What me, a mere six-day member who hardy ever played in competitions because he was usually engaged in weekend activities in the mistress bedroom and who has never won a trophy on his own account? And what me, the man who spends more time propping up the bar telling deeds of derring-do rather than performing them? No wonder Niblick was perplexed.

At first, Mashie Niblick was convinced that the invitation to become the club vice-captain was a hoax perpetrated by one of the "Friday whip night" gang he drinks with, especially as the email address was one of those jumbled messes that maniacs invent. But the more he thought about it, the more he began to realise that he was undoubtedly the last resort, half-decent members having already donned the captain's green jacket and any others shying away from involvement in a position which requires public speaking, fund raising, administrative tasks and, of course, the odd cavorting down the fairways and then holding court at the 19th.

Now Niblick is a past master at propping up bars having been schooled in the art by supreme masters in Fleet Street in days of yore where he also perfected the art of declaiming the poem he wrote in 1978, "Slagheaps of my Youth". It then dawned upon Niblick that his sole qualification for this august role was that he was one of the club's two stalwart boozers, the other being his good mate Terry Insole, who ruled himself out as he was captain in 2004.

The more Niblick considered it, the dafter it seemed. There was Captain Mark Bonham's invitation to the self-styled maverick iconoclast who had reinvented himself as an abstract sculptor in 2009 which showed Mark had more faith in Niblick than Mashie has in his golf. Mark wrote: "You are now a long-standing member of the club, who has worked on the committee before, reliably represented the club at all levels, matches, general play and social events. You are without doubt capable of coping with the 'speaking duties' and would be able to draw on a considerable library of anecdotes to embellish the occasions now that you are a sculptor, poet and piss artiste."

He took that latter line from Niblick's business card and his epic artistic website where Niblick lambasts most of the current crop of British abstract artists and shows that in the bulldust business, Mashie Niblick can compete with any of them. No, he has never sold one artwork as yet, suffered rejections by the sculpture judges at the Royal Academy, but he ploughs on safe in the knowledge that in the end quality will tell as it has done in his vain attempts to get his name listed on those lustrous competition boards. That's it, said Niblick, the only way I am ever going to get my name inscribed in gold on a club honours board is by becoming club captain . . .

Never a one to shirk a challenge, Niblick decided to accept. After all, this could not be as big a disaster as the Nottingham newspaper he and a few mates launched in 1972, which went down the plughole faster than they got copies off the flatbed printing machine. Failure teaches you lessons, claim the successful. What it taught Niblick was that failure is vastly more prevalent than success, though it is only the successful who blow trumpets in the ears of the losers.

It was a muted acceptance. Niblick wrote to Captain Bonham: "It has dawned on me that I am one of the stalwarts of the Bar—the golf club one, not the judicial—and thus have unimpeachable credentials for spending even more time there. So, yes, I will gladly accept your offer to become your current vice-captain and subsequent 2013 Captain, provided the membership will accept that not only will they get a maverick abstract sculptor running the show, but also a golfing joker and joking golfer . . ." A delighted Captain Bonham then urged Niblick to keep the news under his hat until it appeared officially on the club notice board.

Now began the intrigue. The next day Niblick was playing in a seniors' outing at Wanstead's parkland course and after the match that David Quinn and Niblick comprehensively lost, Niblick was putting his clubs back into his battered car when up hove dapper John Peters, the club's immediate past president, and he greeted Niblick effusively, though without once mentioning the subject of which they were both aware.

It was the same on the Monday. Just having deposited his pull trolley and clubs in the shed next to the clubhouse, Niblick spied his sparring partner, committee member Terry Insole in the clubhouse. Terry was totally in the know and immediately accused Niblick of being a turncoat in view of a spat Niblick had against the management committee some years back when he gave up publicising the club. Major Insole even amplified this by despatching a rambling phone text message which read: "There happens amongst us, a rare one, a turncoat of either side. Aye aye, Captain, says he, here I be sir at your request prostituted be I forever for one pint of the house best . . ." Then in the evening booze-up, surrounded by pals ignorant of the imminent announcement, Terry kept on throwing out hints and attempting to get Niblick to reveal all. He declined, even though the roly-poly former Bow Street police station sergeant Mick McShea was lauding Niblick's capabilities and bemoaning the fact that Mashie had never been offered the club captaincy.

And while the vice-captaincy appointment was being promulgated, there was Niblick as the rebel being jogged about at a tantric sex introductory evening in Holloway. It was not Niblick's idea of an evening out, but he was dragged along there by what might loosely be described as the "vice-captain's lady" with the emphasis on the first word. Now the rich folk in the Western world who encounter domestic problems head off to see a psychiatrist; lesser mortals join some oddball outfit like a tantric sex group and find fulfilment, salvation and an answer to their problems. These are the believers and the converts who invest their faith in an idea and benefit immensely.

As someone still enjoying a healthy and positive outlook on life, Niblick had no need for a fillip from this technique and made this plain to the 40 or so acolytes. Indeed, when he had to fill in the questionnaire as to how matters had gone, Niblick rated the best part of the evening as the coffee break. The surprise to Niblick was that after the event, when clearly he was the sole deviant who challenged the status quo, various women came up to him attempting to lure him back for further sessions. One slim, grey-haired widow who announced that she was "back in the dating business" told Niblick that her late architect husband had been a sceptic like Mashie but once he acknowledged that there was some underlying truth in the tantric system, they went on to enjoy "fantastic sex". Niblick said that he was amazed that anyone could be so blatantly optimistic.

The notice announcing Niblick's acceptance of the vice-captaincy went up on the club board on July 5, 2012 and resulted in handshakes all around from pals keeping the barrels turning, even including that sceptic Terry Insole, when Mashie showed up at the club in the evening. The impression Niblick got was that the lads from the "Friday night whip gang" were pleased to see one of their own placed in a position of authority, someone attuned to their needs and aspirations.

There were congratulations and the odd commiseration from other members when the word got around and then Niblick was bombarded with advice on what to do in the captain's role. Firstly, Captain Bonham met him in the bar to explain what his duties would be—chairing the monthly management committee meetings, nominating the captains of teams for various inter-club competitions, leading the lads playing in captain's friendly matches, which, incidentally always end in "honourable draws" and, of course, being the chief club mourner at the funerals of aged members. Then the club president, Peter Willett, advised Niblick always to listen to the moans of members, even, maybe when nothing positive could be achieved from being this sounding board.

The nitty gritty came at the management committee meetings as Niblick re-discovered in August, 2012. What to do about one long-time member who lost his temper when a competition ruling went against him and he stormed off the green and out of the competition? What to do about the falling membership, the lifeblood of the club? How to attract more green fee payers to the course after one of the wettest summers in living memory? Problems, problems, problems . . .

Oddly, Mashie Niblick had assumed that the green jacket donned by the captain after his election at the annual meeting was magically produced by the club itself. Oh, no, Mark told Niblick that you have to buy the outfit; his cost under £200 from a back street tailor in Forest Gate. This is a man I must pursue, said Niblick, as going, for example to Savile Row, would cost a damn sight more.

Now in making these observations, Niblick saw himself as the everyday golfer who has a remarkable scoring round on one day in the year and rubbish scores on the other 364 days. "So I'm really Captain Crap," Niblick remarked, "but that's perhaps straining credulity a shade since I once upon a time shot a fluke hole-in-one at Maylands GC, at Havering in east London". In Fleet Street Niblick was "The Gaffer", so dubbed by a Mansfield Woodhouse miner dad of a workmate; at the golf club, he became known as "Vice" though there are people who would love to call him Captain Bullshit because of his propensity to use the word.

The golf club itself is neither posh like St Andrews in Fife, nor municipal, like St Andrews in Fife. It is a somewhat middling outfit, a private club itself but beholden to the City of London Corporation on whose ancient woodland it plays for a modest rent. A nine-hole course where you have to play in either a red top or red trousers, it has a good bit more autonomy than some others in similar circumstances. But because it is on publicly-owned land, any Tom, Dick or Harriet can walk their dogs across the bunkerless course—and they do, often outnumbering golfers, resulting in one wag labelling it "dog-shit alley".

That label is a touch over the top because the course is no parkland ramble but a really tough test for most high handicap golfers; Niblick's first taste of it in the late 1990s resulted in his out-driving all his fellow partners on a taster outing and losing 12 balls in the process over 18 holes. Describing it in a couple of words, Niblick called it a "jungle course" because of the dense vegetation beneath the trees that line every hole. You will do reasonably well if you can hit a straight ball and stick to the fairways, but badly if you are wayward with your shots and play zig-zag golf like Niblick is prone to do. Niblick averages losing four balls a round; when he manages to complete 18 holes with the same ball, he gives thanks to St Dunlop or the well-endowed angel Top Flite.

The clubhouse is separated from the course by a suburban road and somewhat set back; so shy is it of being boastful that scores of folk living nearby do not know of its existence. Yet it is a pleasant place boasting a pro's shop, small locker rooms and showers plus the usual bar and dining area often used by folk celebrating birthdays and the like. The greenkeepers have their own shed area to park tractors and farming tools for use in their lost cause of keeping the explosive arboreal growth at bay. But at least they treat the greens as virgins to be pampered and coaxed to a winsome state. Most visiting club golfers laud the greens to the skies even when they cannot read them.

The members are a mixed lot, mainly modestly well-off, butchers, bakers, cabbies and candlestick makers and all the trades and professions in between; indeed, Clement Attlee, the Labour MP who later became Prime Minister and who had lived in the area, was once a member. These members display the characteristics seen at every club in the land: the long hitters, the deadly putters, the boasters, the wastrels, the tightwads and, of course, the occasional cheat.

None of them though, in Niblick's experience, is as blatantly nefarious as one businessman Niblick regularly caddied for at the Notts Golf Club at Hollinwell, Kirkby-in-Ashfield, in the 1950s. This chap, Charlie the Cheat, would always play with a Dunlop 65 ball with the number 5 on it and he regularly changed his balls so that they were always gleaming. Niblick was smartly informed by Charlie that when the caddy spotted Charlie's ball in a dodgy lie, Niblick was to bend down to tie his shoelace and surreptitiously pocket the ball. After a wink or a nod from Niblick, his master ambled off in the general vicinity, secretly retrieved another No 5 ball from his right-hand trouser pocket and slipped it down his left-side pocket which had a large hole in it. In mock surprise, the master would shout out "I've got it".

For assisting in this cheating enterprise, Niblick was rewarded with six shillings pay for an 18-hole bag-carrying round which normally paid five bob. Wages of sin they may have been but they taught Niblick that there's a lot more grey than black or white in golf or any other enterprise.

Niblick therefore had a perceptive introduction to this strange world of golf. With the dedication that Niblick's brother Nick showed, he might—and I heavily stress the word "might"—have gone on to fame and fortune . . . But while brother was spending summer afternoons perfecting his 6-iron play on the practice ground at Coxmoor GC, Sutton-in-Ashfield, Niblick was consorting with the greenkeeper's nubile daughter. Brother finished up with a handicap of four after competing in the British Boys' championship; Niblick with a handicap of 24. Who had the better deal? These days most people questioned come down heavily in favour of Niblick, though admittedly his supporters are also high handicap martyrs to the game.

In Niblick's mind, the club is the nearest in England to those all-inclusive Scottish golf clubs, like Scotscraig in Fife, where there seem to be no rigid class or social divides. Niblick has come across a village roadsweeper in Scotland who is venerated by his club mates ranging from businessmen to doctors as he is a damned good golfer. But then golf, as one brawny Scot informed Niblick, is the Scottish national sport. Would that this were more the case in England where class divisions are rife. Still there are some other English golf clubs with a decent outlook and one in particular that springs to mind is Whitewebbs at Enfield. There a magical bunch of lads still have their own shabby clubhouse on a testing council course and welcome rival club parties with open arms. The plain English fare served up after a captain's friendly match is mouth-wateringly good. It is Niblick's favourite local golf outing of the year.

Now the full extent of the folly in choosing Niblick to be the 2013 captain came with his first outing in a Saturday October medal. He shot a score of 129, not over 36 holes as Rory McIlroy might do, but over the regulation 18. Niblick did pull a muscle in his back when coming off the first, but never the one for facile excuses, he attributed his failings to three bad holes when he clocked two 10s and a 13, the latter tally after landing in an area of ancient anthills with Corporation preservation orders on them. They just kept on defying wild swings with a sand iron. In the end he had to ask himself the question he put to a pal who had landed in a similar hazard: "Just ask yourself which silly idiot put the ball there . . ."

Yet when the scores went up for Division 2 competitors, Niblick relished the fact that although he might be "Honest John" in entering such a lousy card, there were four more anti-heroes who were so disgusted with their play that they did not even return a scorecard despite paying £3 into the competition pot. Niblick was thus bottom of the scoring heap yet could look down sneeringly on the shamefaced foursome unable to acknowledge their ineptness.

Niblick's golfing incompetence was again highlighted in the Tigers, Foxes and Rabbits competition when he was soundly beaten 5 & 4 by Captain Bonham of the Tigers team of low handicap players as well as Peter Willett, the club secretary, representing the mid-ranking Foxes. Willett won by 3 & 2. Still Niblick claimed his game had marginally improved because he lost only three balls to the wicked slice he had developed.

Matters were much better on the drive-in front. A good month before the annual captain's drive-in, Niblick had decided to write a modest playlet to be performed by Mashie Niblick's team decked out as Robin Hood and his Merry men. Niblick had already purchased a hunting horn for this purpose and he envisaged the lads, plus female camp followers, exiting the clubhouse to the sound of the horn blasts and the singing of the Robin Hood TV theme song as they headed for the 10th tee.

The playlet, a sort of mixture of Monty Python and the Goodies, would end with the firing of toy bows and rubber-suction tipped arrows. There were several tweaks to the script and in particular, Major Insole came up with the bright idea that Robin Hood as played by Captain Niblick should ride on a hobby horse. Niblick also had the notion that this remarkable spectacle should not just be restricted to golfers and other fellow travellers, but should be broadcast more widely. Hence his decision to contact the local news editors for the various TV stations in the capital. After all, Sunday is usually a slack day for news and a 2 minutes 47 seconds comedy show would liven up their news bulletins.

Shock and awe was the aim of newly-elected Captain Mashie Niblick at his inaugural drive-in at the golf club; surprise and amazement there certainly was.

Dressed as Robin Hood with a team of Merry Men supporting him, the Captain blew blasts on a hunting horn as he rode his hobby horse Woody on to the greensward masquerading as the 10th tee. There then followed a three-minute comedy sketch in the eccentric tradition of the club's drives-in to office.

The sketch had a couple of hitches in it with David of Doncaster, always a loose cannon, setting off to the tee five minutes before the rest of the Outlaws and Will Scarlett being stumped when Robin addressed him by his proper name. But, opined Niblick, an audience like this one, made up mainly of golfers, always expects a cock-up or two and this adds to the spectacle.

The idea, said Captain Niblick, was to show those itinerant golfers who wander from golf course to golf course lured by the blandishments of a free breakfast here or free lunch there, what they are missing by not being members of a golf club.

"Peripatetic golfers have a platonic relationship with the courses they play. Proper club golfers have a much deeper relationship, almost akin to marriage". He said that the comradeship and companionship you get as a golf club member was self-evident in the enthusiasm displayed by his pals who made up the team of Merry Men alongside Maid Marian, Mistress Karen and the sheriff's kidnapped daughter, Cheryl of Nottingham.

Under their Lincoln Green tabards, the team leader (one Mashie Niblick) was highly inventive in creating their costumes with Will Scarlett carrying a mock iPad mini and wearing a miner's lamp; Alan A'Dale strumming a ukelele; George A'Green, the forest jester doing a diddly-dum, diddly-dee refrain in his multi-coloured jester's hat; David of Doncaster wearing a real jockey's cap; Little John in giant boots with mock toes sticking out of them with the rest in outlandish garb. A late arrival after his horse went lame on the ride from Mansfield to Epping Forest was Hobo, the Sherwood ruffian. He appeared on the 10th tee wearing suspenders and fishnet stockings underneath his tabard to the astonishment of spectators. The sketch was performed by the Red Army ensemble—a reference to golfers in the forest being obliged to wear a prominent item of red clothing.

Members with long memories said that they had never seen a drive-in as extravagant as this one at the club. There have been many odd ones, such as the Pearly King, the Victorian cabbie and the Roman emperor with his exploding golf ball.

Captain Niblick said he first had the idea of appearing as Robin Hood because he was born at Retford and raised in Mansfield, the centre of Sherwood Forest. The legend had been with him right through childhood and especially at the time he lived as a baby in Edwinstowe village near the Major Oak and was read the tales of the legend by his mother. From that single idea, it grew into a collective piece with the addition of the Merry Men. There must, Niblick said to himself, be something that the whole caboodle could focus on; hence the Outlaw sketch which he wrote inside an hour.

It was based on the premise that Robin Hood invented communism centuries before Karl Marx had the idea or the poetic pantisocracies dreamed up by Coleridge and his fellow travellers blossomed and quickly failed. This was patently obvious in the written script, though effectively hidden in the oral version because of the play on words—marksmen becoming Marxmen.

But talking of labour and pay, said Captain Niblick, you only get out what you put in. So the Captain paid for the costumes, his lady ran up the tabards, but Niblick declined totally to fund the suspenders and stockings worn by that exhibitionist Hobo. Then there were the caterer's fees for filling the lads up with bacon butties at the crack of dawn plus two decent bottles of single malt whisky to wake up their systems. Also there was the afternoon music session provided by Jingles who did have the decency to turn off the record player while Niblick, wearing his newly-minted Captain's green jacket, gave a rousing rendition of his 1978 poem, The "Slagheaps of My Youth."

It is worth noting the words of this poem because Niblick recites them at almost every opportunity and he does have to emphasise the mistaken impression that crosses most people's minds that these slagheaps were ladies of ill repute. Not a bit of it; they were Mansfield's mountains in 1978. So here goes . . .

Flanked by her captors, Lady Karen (left) and Maid Marian, the fiddler on the hoof, the manacled and black-clad Cheryl of Nottingham is marched to meet her fate accompanied by Friar Tuck

THE SLAGHEAPS OF MY YOUTH

They're taking away the slagheaps
From the landscape of my youth
Murdering all those mountains
Of blood and sweat and booze
To titivate the countryside,
Emasculate grim charm
By erecting fancy hillocks
Of bushes, grass and gorse

Buttymen built those pit tips,
Raised them high with pride
Made them into monuments
To miners who had died
Towering over churches,
Mocking factory spires
Dominating Nottinghamshire
Like Angels in graveyards

If they want fancy countryside
They've got the Yorkshire Dales,
The Derby Peak, the Norfolk Broads
And weatherbeaten Wales
So leave alone my slagheaps
Let them smoke and steam,
Let them boast their living scars
To Hell with prettifying folk

Now in the late 1970s, Niblick despatched this poem to every extant cultural magazine and got the heave-ho from every single one. It is astonishing, he remarked at the time, how many so-called educated types cannot recognise genius when it is staring them straight in the face. Nevertheless the epic poem— "sheer genius" was the description of it by one eminent Fleet Street reporter—became a hallowed tradition when it was annually recited at the Daily Telegraph sub-editors' Christmas lunch held in Ye Olde Cheshire Cheese, Wine Office Court, City, or latterly at The Grapes public house, Narrow Street, Limehouse, when the gallant half-cut Captain had to shove off inebriated diners trying to force knives and forks down his trousers while he was in full spate.

*   *   *

Though it was frosty for the drive-in, it stayed dry and the sun appeared at one point, presaging hopefully a much sunnier golfing year than the foul wet spring, summer and autumn of 2012. The actual drive-in by Robin Hood was an anti-climax. Despite his using a wooden driver as a lad when a member of Coxmoor GC, Sutton-in-Ashfield, and even taking five clubs with wooden heads for practice shots at a local driving range the week before, the leading forest Outlaw scuffed his drive into office and it meandered a mere 32 yards. "Pity I'm not as adept with a wooden driver as I am with a wooden longbow" remarked Robin Hood of the ancient club which resides for the rest of the year in a special place above the clubhouse bar. Members bet money on a sweep to estimate the distance the Captain's drive went and one man even bet on the box listed as "Captain falls off tee". It was a fair bet, as Niblick attested.

"Ah well", said Niblick having shed his Robin Hood garb, "I was more concerned about getting the comedy sketch performed than concentrating on the drive." It later transpired that a previous captain, who shall remain nameless, revealed to Niblick that in the five weeks afore his own inauguration, he had sneaked up to the clubhouse in the early morning, removed the wooden-shafted driver from its resting place and practised with it before craftily returning it to its normal abode. It takes all sorts to make a world, said Niblick, among them rogues and vagabonds.

As if to emphasise his golfing ineptitude, Niblick teed off in the ensuing Texas Scramble competition playing alongside the cream of the club's officers and smote his ball into the nearby starboard trees. He had one grandson as chief caddy pulling Niblick's trolley, plus two more grandchildren as ball spotters. Not one of them could find the ball. Typical of Niblick not only to cock-up his important drive-in on which much money was laid out in a sweep, but then to compound the disaster by losing his ball on his first competitive drive as Captain. His team racked up a respectable total but were well adrift of the winners.

Niblick entertained all his offspring and quite a few of their children to lunch before getting the entertainer Jingles to provide an afternoon and evening of music for dancing. Astonishingly, a number of his younger pals' wives came up to Niblick to congratulate him on his endless energy since Niblick was up and down regularly on the dance floor, though, as some folk observed, with frequent cat-naps in between. Anna Maris even went so far as to reveal the secret of Niblick's dancing routine; "you do the same bloody movements whatever the music," she observed. Getting away with with this for decades, Niblick realised that he had finally been rumbled.

On a slack-news Sunday, all the television news teams as well as the national papers effectively indicated to Niblick that he should jump into the pond next to the 9th tee as they studiously spurned his invitations to film the amazing comedy sketch. The two local organs liked the prospect, but declined to send either photographers or reporters to witness the gallivanting.

And so, as he had fully expected, Niblick sat down the following morning and drafted different versions of the drive-in event for the two newspapers and sent them two pictures each. To his absolute chagrin, no images appeared in print, although one organ did have the grace to stick an image on its internet site. There were reports of the golf, but barely a mention of Robin Hood and the Merry Men cavorting across the greensward. When he complained to editorial bosses, they cited a shortage of space, though one editor, Tim Jones, did promise to run the story in the next issue—a promise he kept. But Niblick rued the fact that some of the previous captains' incarnations he himself had written about got vastly more coverage in local newspapers than his own epic. He observed to the Captain's Lady: "I will rectify this by writing a book about a year in the life of a golf club captain. Then these dozy buggers will realise that they got it drastically wrong."

After that, Captain Mashie Niblick and his lady, the Maid Marian, attended their first official function, the dinner-dance of Theydon Bois GC, in the land of grass-snakes and wild deer. "I'd have much rather gone to the Theydon Girls do than the Bois," observed Niblick after being welcomed by Captain Mike Blagdon and his wife Anne on a wet and windy evening.

The glory of being a club captain is that you are always placed on the top table and get served ahead of all the others. It reminded Niblick of his first outing to a public dinner on a lowly table as a cub reporter in Mansfield when a waitress asked him whether he wanted apple crumble as a sweet or jam pudding. "Apple crumble," replied Niblick. "That's only for the top table," she retorted.

His second public outing of those days was even worse. The organisers of the Sutton-in-Ashfield Liberal Club's angling section welcomed him with open arms as they had no idea how to run a dinner and expected Niblick to know the ropes. Niblick did his best but was blatantly ignored since those fishing lads lit up their fags—this was in an age before political correctness was invented and you could puff away almost anywhere—immediately after they had supped their soup and two courses ahead of the loyal toast and its admonition: "Gentlemen, you may smoke."

They know how to do things at rural Theydon. Niblick was not Niblick but the name of his club, as was young Chingford skipper Mark Arkell, who was known to the top table as Chingford. But then, you are representing your club and it is not all that many generations ago that peasants were known as Percy Chester or Walter Ramsbottom, for example if they hailed from Chester and Ramsbottom.

Niblick was to a small degree handicapped because his lady had twisted her ankle on a walk to the railway station five days before and she had only just shed her crutches. She arrived leaning on a walking stick and was thus unable to indulge in one of her favourite activities, dancing. This, however, was no barrier to Niblick. In between glasses of honest English real ale, he managed to get Leeanne Arkell and Anne Blagdon on to the dance floor as well as Barbara Noble, who only minutes before had collapsed in a heap while energetically dancing.

On the Monday night when Niblick had expected the lads to inquire how he had got on with the Theydon crew, he was put on the spot. "Where was the Captain yesterday?," they demanded to know. Well, said Niblick, the Captain was at the European Doctors' Orchestra concert at the Cadogan Hall near Sloane Square. "The Captain should have been at the club," they retorted. "It is a long-standing tradition that the Captain plays nine holes in the swindle and then moves around the bar in his green blazer with its badge of office chatting to all and sundry." Nobody told me that, said Niblick. "And it would have been a bloody sight cheaper—Maid Marian paid £25 for each for our tickets to see two of her pals perform with the orchestra." Niblick later established from the 2012 Captain Mark Bonham that the Captain was not obliged to attend the Sunday sessions, though Mark had done so regularly.

Negotiating the minefields of officialdom is one thing, putting in a decent performance on the course is quite another. Having enjoyed the demon drink perhaps a little excessively the night before, Niblick needed nine holes to sober up in the December medal. So from three stableford points on the first nine, he garnered another 11 on the second nine to finish absolute bottom in the standings. He reckoned that a teetotal Saturday would see him recover on the Sunday swindle only to register "null points" over nine holes losing four balls into the bargain. This was not the way it was supposed to be.

It became a hat-trick of bottom placings at the Turkey trot event. Niblick reckoned that after losing four balls on the first five holes of a course inundated with dead leaves, especially in those ditches where his ball always seemed to gravitate, he was back in contention alongside partner Paul Verney being boosted by competing against long-hitting club champion Mike Everitt and his steady pal Roger Newman. Taking a leaf out of their book, Niblick never lost another ball on the greensome stableford round and he and Paul accumulated what Niblick considered to be a respectable score of 22 points against the 10 more secured by their rivals. Tail-end Charlies again, and not only that; so poor was his form in the past few outings that his handicap had now gone up by one shot to 27—just one short of the figure that absolute novices play off. He never, in his wildest nightmares, ever expected that the chains of office would weigh down so heavily on his form, which admittedly had been somewhat inconsistent over the last five years. He decided there and then that he needed more tuition from club pro Adam Baker.

"At least you are consistent," observed Maid Marian when told of his abject failures in competitive golf. She was reminded of her brother's attempts in the America's Cup one year. The boat on which he was crewing had been second to last in every single race.

Wealthy golf clubs have teams of employees to keep the courses up to scratch; hard-up ones rely on members to help the couple of greens staff stop the onward march of self-set saplings and rampant holly bushes that endeavour to swamp the outer environs of the rough. So Niblick set off with half a dozen fellow members to carry brambles galore, chopped-back vegetation and sundry other bits of wood to a bonfire of the inanities behind the third green. There were two huge piles of vegetation which, in the end, Niblick volunteered to pile on to a petrol-soaked fire. One novelty was to get a member using the leaf blower to bolster the flames. It worked brilliantly.

Mind you, it was one of those winter mornings when the BBC weather forecaster confidently assured early listeners that it would not rain. It rained. And not only did it rain sometime after Niblick, putting his faith in the weather folk, left the clubhouse without any of the rainwear from his golf bag, but he also managed to put his foot in a puddle which looked shallow on a horse ride but turned out to be an optical illusion. The water went up to his ankle and filled his right shoe.

Never a one to let minuscule setbacks ruin his day, Niblick got stuck in to turning the adjacent fourth fairway into a no-go zone as clouds of smoke obscured 50 yards of the greensward. "Where do you get all your energy from?" inquired fellow bonfire stacker Stuart Runciman, the head greenkeeper. "I've never seen anything like it for a man of your advanced years."

"All down to attitude," Niblick responded. "I have a zest for life and recognise that despite all the blandishments of various religious zealots promising nirvana in the next life, we pass this way once and so we have to make the best of it. That is just what I am doing. You are better off finishing bottom of the pile in a medal than not competing because you are brown bread".

Stuart listened to the Captain's words of wisdom before observing: "I just hope that I'm as lively as you once I retire next year." Half the volunteers went to remove the dense undergrowth beneath oak trees on the starboard side of the fourth fairway and there they found 62 lost balls. "How about auctioning them off," suggested one volunteer. "Be buggered," said Niblick. "Half of them are mine".

A big feature of the club for Niblick is the Friday "whip night" where the lads put a tenner—sometimes more—on the whip card and drink until the card cash is exhausted when they fill it up again. And on the Friday before Christmas when a trip out to a curry house was booked, Niblick decided to face up to the fact that he is inevitably becoming bald, just like his father. So he instructed the lawyer-barber Indie from Croatia at her shop near the tube station to cut the hair on the top of his head short. The whip crew were amazed. It makes you look younger, they told Niblick. "It's knocked ten years off your age," said one wag. "Now you look only 84." Niblick is 74 . . .

He was not the only one to nod off after a skinfull of ale and a hot curry, and fortunately Niblick early on persuaded the "whip" mob's wine connoisseur, the dapper Paul King, who judges wine by the bottle price—"costlier equals better" is his yardstick—to stick to house red. In the past, when taste buds have been shattered at the bar, this tycoon has been known to order wine costing £46 a bottle that tastes like toffee to jaded lips in a local Italian restaurant.

As the year end arrived, Niblick played his last game in 2012, the Sunday whip, where as club Captain, he had the honour of teeing off first. That was the only time he did have the honour and, as usual, he finished bottom of the scoring heap. The final ignominy was that, in trying a new grip— "Guaranteed to make you hit the ball straighter" was the lying message on the internet video—he scuffed his drive into nearby bushes, took three more shots to get out and after zig-zag play eventually finished up on the green with a short putt for a hopeless 12 in 2012. He missed the putt, thus scoring a premature 13 just days before 2013 dawned.

Mashie Niblick then admitted to himself, he later related, that he must now be the world's worst golf club Captain in playing terms and discounting those reprobates—and there have been a goodly number of them across the land—who have run off with the slimline club barmaid or illegally serviced the Lady Captain . . .

Christmas came and went in an alcoholic blur and Niblick faced up to the New Year of 2013—the date on his Captain's blazer was now fully operative—with renewed confidence. This was instantly ruined by two more tail-end Charlie results. There was only one solution to this problem, said Niblick: a lesson from the club professional, Adam Baker.

So, on a chilly Monday morning, Niblick was on the 10th tee having his action vetted by young Adam Baker. It's your wrist action, proclaimed the expert. "You are not breaking your wrists early enough. Your action otherwise is fine." Niblick took the instruction to heart and was soon hitting straighter—and longer—drives, even with a brassie—he refuses to acknowledge these new-fangled names about loft degrees and rescue clubs; they are still driver as the No 1 wood; brassie as the 2 and spoon as the 3 wood in Niblick's lexicon.

So there was a sparkle in Niblick's eyes after this. For a mere £20, the cost of the lesson, he had cured his slice and was ready to take on, perhaps not the world, but maybe the lads in the club's second division, those with handicaps of 15 and above. That he did in the January medal, doubling his score from 10 stableford points on his previous outing to 20 points now. However he still reckoned he was last again even though there were three golfers below him so ashamed of their own scores that they declined to put in cards.

Just as the cynics say once a criminal, always a criminal, Niblick averred that he had no belief in prison reform. Recidivism was indisputable, he said, little realising that the same would apply to his golf improvement. The first Sunday swindle he entered showed him back to his slicing routine. The trouble was that his first drive was hooked into the woods and thereafter, Niblick was always lifting his head too soon to see where the ball was going. Outcome, three more lost balls and tail-end Charlie yet again.

One of his partners, the 1995 Captain Brian Holmes mentioned that in attending the 54th Golfing Society dinner at Wanstead in February, Niblick was down to make a speech on behalf of the guests. This was the first Niblick had heard of this, but he would get by.

Now the golf course is one thing; club politics yet another. Niblick had volunteered to chair the monthly management meetings little realising that these could engender violent views on topics such as the contract details for various staff, whose beer should be served behind the bar, indeed whether or not the tees for the second and 18th holes, which are near to one another, should be switched. He was astonished how vehemently some members held views on these various topics, yet tried to chart a sane course between conflicting parties. Most of the membership had little idea of these slanging matches which ate into drinking time at the nearest pub because the club bar had long since shut. And yet, Niblick had to bend his ear to listen to complaints from members about how visitors who had hired the clubhouse for an evening had left drawing pins in the sliding doors and other such frivolous whinges. A sounding board for the mardy-arsed, a leader of men and a lousy golfer, that is how Niblick viewed himself after two months in the job—and two slack months when funerals and crap golf held sway.

It was "Morning Captain" here, "let the Captain have the honour" there and Captain This and Captain That as members tried to butter up to what Niblick actually described himself as: Captain Crap.

There was a modest respite when Captain Mashie Niblick celebrated his 75th birthday in mid-January. The seniors' section were holding their 2012 December Medal, called off originally because of inclement weather.

Due out first in a three-ball at 8.20am, he was up at 6.30am as for once he was not delayed by having a female partner to warm the cockles of his heart—and other bits too—and was on the first tee practising his iron play five minutes before the off. No-one else showed up, so Niblick ambled back to the clubhouse to find out why the world had turned upside down. Greenkeeper Stuart Runciman told Niblick that the top four holes on a severely frosty morning were unplayable. So that was it: competition off. Nevertheless it took another ten minutes for the head honchos of the seniors' section to acknowledge this. "Well I'm going out to play the bottom five," Niblick announced to the small gathering sipping tea in the clubhouse. No-one took him up on his offer, so Niblick headed off on his own and played ten holes on the frozen surface, clocking up two pars and losing just one ball—much better than his normal summer play. "I would have played 20 holes had not my fingers developed early indications of frostbite," Niblick opined.

Now his former employers, the Telegraph group, regularly put out special offers to subscribers, all of which he had studiously ignored. That is until an offer to dine in the Savoy Hotel's River restaurant for a discounted £35 a head came up. He reasoned that that would not be a bad way of celebrating his three-quarters of a century in this world and promptly ordered two vouchers and fixed up to dine there with Maid Marian on his birthday. He had been before to this notable Strand hotel, way way back in 1965 when Sir Colin Coote retired as Daily Telegraph editor and the newspaper management invited all editorial staff to lunch there. What Niblick remembered about this ancient gathering was that it started him smoking again because foot-long cigars were offered to all and sundry at the end of the meal. He could not ignore that generous offer and so fell foul again of the dreaded weed well before he gave it up again when he married a former Olympic runner and one-time world record holder over 1500 metres.

Now the Savoy does one thing extremely well; it mollycoddles its diners. So after a pleasant meal of food on a plate you would have thought had been designed by Picasso, a waiter showed up with a dish containing six small bon-bons and an ornate message inscribed in chocolate: "Happy Birthday". Not only that, but when Niblick departed the restaurant, the maitre d'hotel wished him by name a happy rest of his birthday. Little did the suave chap realise that the £35 cost of one three-course meal was the same price as the Asda store suit that Niblick wore to the event . . .

Of course, the lads at the club were delighted to take the mickey. Colin Thompson sent an email saying that he had heard that Maid Marian and the Captain were going out for saveloys. "Enjoy your saveloys meal," he wrote.

On the other side of the coin, there was latent anger among various committee members concerning contracts for various folk which some wanted rejigged. Niblick said he always found it interesting to note how keen some folk were to lay down the law and instruct others on ways of working in which they themselves were deficient. Fine, Niblick told his fellow committee members, to set ambitious targets that were clearly unattainable without acknowledging human frailties. We can strive for perfection, yet we never can achieve it, he remarked. "Always recognise that despite abundant talent around, it is so easy to ignore the mundane jobs that people carry out that enable the rest of us to prosper". Events do not organise themselves, they need massive input from the humble hewers of wood and drawers of water.

January snow put paid to golf and to committee work, though some managed to exploit the email system to get their views across. With his playing partner John Walker due to go away on a sunshine holiday, there was pressure on him and the Captain to finish the first round of the L G Jeffrey Trophy before the predicted snow storms hit Britain.

With the top four holes deemed unplayable, the four-ball settled on doing the bottom five a number of times as sleet gently fell. Soon it was swirling sleet so that Brian Meggs, Phil Gauci, John Walker and the

Captain resembled the Four Golfers of the Apocalypse, battered by the sleet, losing balls in the gloaming and trying valiantly to putt on frozen greens that resembled concrete flooring. Mad dogs—there were numerous pooch-walkers on the course—and gormless golfers go out in the mid-day snow was how Niblick saw it. By mutual consent, though here again, the Captain claimed the final word, conditions were so dire that all agreed that the last match in the first round of the trophy competition would be decided over 10 holes. Only nine were needed as the Captain and his mate lost too many balls to stand an earthly chance and their opponents finished three up or, to put it more sensibly, the Captain and his partner finished three down.

Given his lousy golfing record in these early months of his captaincy, Mashie Niblick was able to boast loudly about being the world's worst golf club captain. No-one jibbed at that, though Niblick was surprised to get wind of various members muttering that the club had elected a clueless captain who could neither drive, nor chip nor putt. But there's more to being Captain than shooting bogeys and double bogeys and even triple bogeys, Niblick averred. There's the drinking—Niblick was acknowledged to be in the first division, if not the premier league here—and the speechifying . . . drinking and speechifying and speechifying and drinking. Here he was a leader; indeed the leader in the clubhouse.

The big problem facing the club in 2013 was diminishing membership, according to Niblick. Launched in 1890 on Corporation of London land in Epping Forest, the club thrived in the 20th century—apart from the war years—as more and more people took up the game. Indeed in the 1980s there was a waiting list of golfers wanting to join. They had to pay a £500 joining fee—as did Niblick himself in 1997—and do time as a five-day member before graduating via dead men's shoes to full seven-day membership.

Then came Motorway 25. Almost overnight, a shortage of membership places at the club and at other courses nearby turned turtle as farmers sold off land beside the motorway for golf courses galore, all crying out for members. The club joining fee was scrapped as the slow attrition in membership took hold. For now a new breed of golfers was born: the itinerants. With such a wealth of new courses offering blandishments of "free buggy for four" or "free full English breakfast" to all and sundry whether with handicaps or not, these peripatetic players suddenly found that they were not restricted to the same old holes every week, but could try out a coastal links course here, an urban course there within sight of Canary Wharf. And while the club golfer paid his or her subscription come rain or shine, these green fee itinerants just shopped around when they fancied doing so, largely when the sun was shining. It seemed, for many golf clubs in the Home Counties at least, that the demise of the club golfer was nigh.

How to reverse this trend was the issue of the day. How to achieve this was something that taxed Niblick's ingenuity yet he knew that it was not impossible. But before launching initiatives to recruit new members, the club had to staunch the diminution in the membership roll of golfers quitting the club. There were around five of these quitters at the turn of the year, some departing through ill health as well as the inevitable loss of older members dying off.

None of these quitters will get a mention here, said Niblick. Some he had warned against resigning their membership as they would regret it by the year end when his grand tome on golf was published, not that he alerted them to the book he was getting his amanuensis, JMW, to write as that would alter their standpoint. No, the book project was a secret between Niblick and his amenuensis and, of course, the Captain's Lady.

Niblick had to laugh, though, at one chap's resignation reason. "I shall be working abroad a lot this year, so it is not feasible for me to remain a member; I will switch from being a playing member to being a social member," he told club officials. He lives a 10-minute walk from the club, so why has he gone and joined another golf club 12 miles away . . . . The duplicity of some folk is astonishing, said Niblick.

A more pressing problem at the club was a financial one. Even with the subscription fees rise passed at the annual meeting in November having now kicked in, the increased income was negated by the loss from the fees of these ignoble quitters.

One management committee member even suggested that by dispensing with the services of the professional, the club could save £10,000 annually. This provoked a vehement response by Niblick. Losing the professional was like driving a car without tyres; it would bumble along, but get nowhere, he asserted. Niblick said that he would not want to be a member of a club which had no professional. True their roles had changed from being golf club makers to being epic players in their own rights or assuming the role of teachers. And the club pro was a fine teacher, said Niblick. He was a fallible human being as we all are. So trenchant was his defence of the notion of a pro being the nucleus of any golf club that the committee sided with him. Voting was 7-1 for keeping a professional with one person sitting on the fence and abstaining.

A new deal for the professional was then put in hand with minor changes from his previous contract. But the argument highlighted the cultural clash between the progressives and the reactionaries. It was a theme that would be played out again and again during the year. Niblick made plain that he was for continuity while not abhorring change. For change is inevitable, he said. Stand against change and you are lost, which was why he was advocating the greater use of social network sites such as Facebook to commune with the younger generation. "I can't stand Facebook or Twitter," he told committee members, "but all my offspring and their offspring embrace it so it is up to the club to move with the times."

Of course these disputes between folk with deeply-entrenched views are inevitable. And this is what the ordinary club members remain in the dark about. They can read the monthly minutes but these generally record decisions made without going too deeply in to the issues involved.

Against all this brainstorming there are the lighter moments when sections of the club get together to celebrate. One such was a secret party for the Lady Captain Irene Dupree when she notched up a special birthday. Unbeknown to Irene, her husband Dave circulated golfing friends and relatives asking them to gather at the club before 6.30pm on February 1. Dave told his wife that he was taking her out for a birthday dinner, but needed to call at the club first. He did so, then marched out again telling Irene that club secretary Peter Willett urgently need to talk to her.

While the guests inside the clubhouse stayed quiet, the innocent Irene entered the secretary's office and was then asked if she could step into the dining room. As soon as she opened the door, the astonished woman was greeted by cheers and "Happy Birthday" chants. Dave's ruse had worked an absolute treat and Irene went on to enjoy the most unexpected birthday party of her life.

There are the ups and downs of life in the golf club as in any other business and what my task as captain is to do is to ensure that there are vastly more pluses than minuses, said Niblick. And with that in mind, he and his side-kick Terry Insole decided to promote an afternoon karaoke session by hiring entertainer Jimmy Batten and between them funding Jim's fee so that the event was a free one for members. It quickly built up a bank of punters with nearly 50 souls signing up in the first couple of days that the notice went up.

Meantime, after January snow shut the course for several days, it reopened in time for the February medal, still with areas resembling a quagmire. Niblick lost five balls on his round and for the first time in his tenure as club skipper, he did not finish bottom of the pile. He was next to the bottom. Now his score did modestly improve on previous outings, but Niblick knew at the back of his mind that only a lousy round by Chris Phillips saved him from the ignominy of being last for the seventh time on the trot. He did not accept that things were beginning to look up for him, but they had decidedly begun to look down for the carpet-layer-to-royalty Chris.

The beginning of the year was a gentle introduction to the burdens of the captaincy, though club secretary Peter Willett reckoned that from March onwards, Niblick would not know whether he was coming or going. Things began to pick up in February with the election of John Peters, twice club captain, to the presidency of the county golf union. Here was a true tale of nowhere to somewhere as Peters took up the game after caddying for his next-door neighbour in Leytonstone.

It was one of those glorious tales of a likely lad having the determination to get on and sticking to his last until he reached his goal as the most important golfing individual in Essex and north-east London. Behind the glory of his unanimous election at Upminster, there was the buried agenda of how to shore up affiliated clubs who are shedding members by the score.

The trouble, as Niblick has complained about before, is the trend among today's golfers of not wanting to be restricted to play at one club, but to go where they fancy and just pay green fees. What these lads fail to acknowledge is that the clubs they so despise have yearly arrangements to play each other at home and away at very little cost to the golfers involved; indeed these inter-club matches usually involve a decent meal afterwards, often of steak pie in the honest English food tradition.

Imposter: "Little" John Beecroft tries on the captain's jacket to the amusement of Vice-captain Zekia Alsanjak

There was another problem that emerged at the union's annual meeting, one that had never crossed Niblick's mind: youngsters objected strongly to the Congu handicap system and were decidedly averse to needing to buy or hire dinner suits for club dinners, according to a survey by one golf club. This could be a warped survey as it was certainly conducted on an ad hoc basis.

Michael Foster, the Theydon captain, architect and a decent toper, next contacted Niblick to arrange a meeting to discuss this very issue of the whittling away of 7-day members at many of the clubs in the area. At a lunchtime meeting at The Cricketers pub, they agreed to explore the possibility of a playing agreement between the two clubs.

The one really great piece of news for Captain Mashie Niblick was that in the early days of February, he had nailed his Vice-captain, the Turkish-Cypriot expatriate Zekia Alsanjak, a businessman whom the Queen had honoured with an MBE for his work representing the Turkish-Cypriot community. Now here was a proper golfer. Zek plays off a handicap of 10, gets his name inscribed in gold on the club honours boards and is a thoroughly decent cove, unlike the loudmouth Niblick.

Once he reflected upon this, Niblick began to realise just how lucky he was not only to latch on to a decent vice-captain who would, in the fullness of time, accede to the captaincy, but to do it in mid-February. With so many potential candidates turning down the vice-captaincy in 2012, Niblick acknowledged that he was last man standing, the very last resort when approached in mid-summer. But little did the club's mandarins realise that in Niblick they had got a one-off, someone who immediately propelled the golf club to the forefront with a legion of reports in the local newspapers, and also someone who would make the name of this tinpot nine-hole course resound around the world. For here in the unlikely environs of Epping Forest, there was the world's worst golf captain telling the members in nearly 4,000 golf clubs across the British Isles what the real golf world was like.

Naturally, Zek got the nod from the club's management committee without one dissident voice and Niblick was delighted to pass on the good news to the dapper Turk. All that was required then was to get a photograph of Zek swinging his driver plus a report for the local papers and Zek was on board, delighted to see his name and picture in print. What surprised Niblick was that at 76, Zek was even older than than Niblick himself. As Niblick pertinently observed: "Our vice-captains get more newspaper publicity than the captains of other fancier clubs and all thanks to my reporting."

In an effort to boost club revenue, Niblick got together with his sidekick Terry Insole to promote a karaoke afternoon, which happened to be a day after Terry's birthday. Each contributed £100 for the hire of Jimmy Batten and his musical gear and the session was an outstanding success for the participants with £1,100 being spent behind the bar. And this came the day after one of the most successful Quiz Nights in years. With more than 100 contestants in 11 teams, the club was on the verge of running out of chairs to accommodate everyone.

True, both events brought in modest funds for the club—and by heck they needed the money—yet this was the small beer of club income, what the club needed was a massive injection of funds, preferably by luring more members to the outfit and stemming the slow attrition of golfers leaving. So Niblick turned his hand to writing a welcome note in a club leaflet to all visiting golfers. It was the first modest shell fired in anger in the Captain's armoury. Next would be a giant banner to be placed outside the clubhouse.

Niblick had thought the whole business out. It did not look enticing. The club was, he maintained, facing the biggest crisis in its 113-year history. Just as the High Street chain giants Jessops, HMV and Comet had gone bust by failing to change with the times, so the club was in a similar quandary. True, the number of affiliated clubs in the county golf union had doubled in the last 30 years, so that even with more people than ever before taking up the game, there were now vastly more tee-off times and membership options available than had been the case in the past.

What many folk considered to be its main detraction—the course was only nine holes long—Niblick said should be its principle boast. Many players could not afford four hours to amble around 18 holes in this busy world with work and domestic demands reducing their free time. So, publicise the course as a place to unwind after a stressful day in the City, especially in the long summer evenings. After all, the course, in heavily-populated north-east London, was maybe a 20-30 minute drive from Canary Wharf and locals, like Niblick, could drive there in five minutes. Nearness and availability should be our watchwords, maintained Niblick.

In the meantime, Niblick had been slotted in as a speaker at the male-only annual dinner of the 54th Golfing Society. This was an outfit formed by members of the 54th Regiment Home Guard after the Second World War when the lads then wanted to retain the camaraderie engendered during their army service. These days the society had metamorphosed into a collection of past captains of local golf clubs, still with a military veneer.

While it was hinted to Niblick that in his speech toasting the society on behalf of the guests, he might make reference to the TV hit "Dad's Army", the eccentric maverick that is Mashie Niblick took an entirely different line: he focussed on cheating in golf. The somewhat abashed members heard him out, noting his gesticulations as he told of Charlie the Cheat and the hole in his left-hand trouser pocket. There was polite applause at the conclusion of his litany of various cheating methods—none of which, of course, applied to this august gathering of golfers at Wanstead. Yet Niblick reckoned he had done extremely well to speak without notes after more than three hours of decent drinking with a meal thrown in. The biggest wonder was that he did not fall asleep as was his wont at lengthy boozing sessions.

Finally Niblick decided to place a stick of dynamite under the management committee which was complacently considering changing the membership structure of the club. In the 12 years of the 21st century, captains had come and gone and the only traces of their stints were their captain's blazers brought out at funerals and other special events as well as their names being inscribed in gold on the Captains board. There was one dissident, Terry Insole in 2004, but he was ground down by the establishment and the only impression he made was in boosting green-fee income.

Niblick, a quite determined individual, averred that he would not be the usual placeman. So he drafted a set of proposals which the committee would have to face up to and face up to the awkward truth long swept under the table. After several more drafts, Niblick delivered his bombshell to committee members at the dead of night. This is what it said:

Having carefully studied the various ideas put forward by management committee members of late, I have concluded that we are fiddling while Rome burns. As Captain, I have spent considerable time debating the club's predicament in my own mind and have formulated a set of bold, nay stark plans to put before you.

Lady members Justine Chan and Anna Maris enjoy a tipple at the club bar

RADICAL PROPOSALS FROM THE CAPTAIN

With membership levels in terminal decline, the golf club is facing the gravest crisis in its 113-year history and yet we fail to address the real situation, merely tinkering with membership categories.

Year by year in this century, there has been a gradual attrition of membership totals until we stand today with the lowest membership in our modern history. Unless we take radical measures, this club faces the real prospect of following Comet, HMV and Jessops into oblivion.

The fact is that we have failed like them to move with the times. Society has changed and continues to do so while we still cling to policies that served us well 30 years ago, but are outdated today. There are more golfers in this land than there ever have been before but they don't want to spend maybe £1,000 a year to join a club, preferring a peripatetic and cheaper existence of golfing here, there, and everywhere. True there are twice as many golf clubs in the Essex Golf Union than there were 30 years ago with all of them vying for members and offering blandishments to visiting green-fee golfers. This is something that we have to live with and also something that we can exploit.

Too often, I have heard the moan from some members that "we are only a nine-hole course", a whinge that implies that it is just the 18-hole courses that are worth playing. What we need to do is to boast that we are a tough nine-hole course ideal for time-starved golfers to unwind and get some exercise in glorious surroundings. The working man and woman, perhaps with family commitments, often finds that a round of 18 holes taking four to five hours is too much time to selfishly devote to one sport. We need to sell them the idea that a two-hour ramble over nine holes is the solution.

We also need to revise our dress codes. We should inform visitors that they can play in jeans and golf shoes as long as they have a red jumper or shirt which does not have to have a collar; that trainers, jeans and t-shirts are eminently acceptable in the clubhouse. If you look around at young men and women today, they mostly wear jeans, t-shirts and trainers and because of the range of golf courses available to them, they will shun clubs with petty dress restrictions. They are the sartorial pipers calling the tunes.

Our future in the changed social and financial situation in which we find ourselves is, I believe, firstly to go hell-for-leather to attract green-fee payers to the course, boasting of our competitive charges and our accessibility. If we retain the nucleus of the membership we now have, green fees may well stave off an imminent demise. Green-fee income has kept this club afloat in the 21st century. We need to shed the notion, which did once apply generally and still does among some veterans, that this is a members' club first and foremost and green fees are an awkward appendage.

One other thing: we have to police the golf course properly as too many bandits are slipping in without paying the club a penny piece. Some years ago when Alan Spicer went out on a sunny bank holiday as solo course marshal, he collected £400 from bilkers on that single day. That is an indication of the extent to which we are failing in our duty to collect dues from these bandits, who well know how lax is our policing. As I have long maintained, we need to buy an electric buggy—I priced a used one this week at £1,450 plus VAT—paint the words "course marshal" on it and get volunteers to man it regularly. It will pay for itself in no time and then we can consider employing pensioners at modest cost to do this vital task.

In the year 2000, we had 144 seven-day playing members, 81 five-day members, 103 juniors and 47 lady members, giving a grand total of 272 adult players according to listings in that year's diary. Today, our latest January figures state this: 53 seven-day members, 28 six-day, 21 lady members, 35 associate members and 34 juniors, giving us a total of 134 adult players. Over 12 years we have lost half of our adult playing members.

Those missing golfers haven't all died, most of them have walked away. And so we have this vicious circle: members leave mainly because subscriptions rise; we increase subscriptions to balance the books and thus more members disappear. It has happened just about every year this century. So how do we combat this terminal decline? My drastic answer is to build a cushion of capital by deliberately going all out for green-fee income—including cash from the dodgers mentioned above—and then by slashing our membership fees during these straitened times. If we set an annual subscription of £699 for all members, whether seven or six-day players, I reckon that we could not only stem the annual attrition, but actually begin to increase our membership. I would rather see 200 members paying at this rate than the paltry 134 paying up to £927 annually. In simple terms, we would earn more income from 200 members paying £699 annual fees than we get from our present subscription system. I applaud the Tesco motto of "pile it high, sell it cheap". Just work it out. Your cash-strapped father who can manage only to golf on Saturdays is now paying £17.82 a round for the privilege of using the course 52 days a year, which is more expensive than a weekend green fee. That is ridiculous. We have to act and act now to rescue the club. Sure, it is a gamble, but I do not want to be the captain presiding over the club's slow but seemingly inevitable demise.

This is not the road to ruin; it is the road to salvation. This gamble has been tried already at the fairly new rural club at Epping. There on a restricted membership, the owner levies a joining fee of £40 plus an annual subscription of £295 giving members half-price green fees (the going full 18-hole rates are green fees of £14 midweek and £21 weekends). There is a membership waiting list at noisy Epping—it is beside both the M11 and M25—and I recently asked the owner, Neil Sjoberg, how he managed to do it. It was, he said, his livelihood; if he didn't make money out of it he would lose his house and weekly "wages". That was incentive enough for him to think outside the box. The hook, clearly, is the low £295 membership fee because if you want unlimited fee-free golf, you have to pay another £450. That would bring the annual first year cost to £785, made up of the £40 joining fee, £295 subscription and £450 for a season ticket of no green fees. His clever system works, though I do not think we could adequately replicate it as our course is on public land and therefore open to all comers and not properly policed. Given the distaste among some of our golfers for green-fee visitors at a members' club, I cannot see our members agreeing to pay extra green fees.

We are already on the way to lifting our profile locally by ordering a banner to denote prominently where we are based. Other publicity aspects are in the process of being addressed. One thing that I personally would espouse is the opening of the gate to the course—once we have dry weather conditions—so that members and visitors regularly can use the overflow car park near the 10th tee. Too many times, I have heard complaints from visiting golfers playing here in friendly matches who have had to park half a mile up the road because parents of children at the adjacent school have filled up the car park. This would be an easy task; all we have to do is to get the greens staff to place the "overflow golfers' parking" sign up there.

To me, the current membership categories are adequate. You can start as a novice on our £200 package and go on from there. There are quite enough membership options available without complicating matters further by introducing more, though if we go the way of my suggested gamble, these charges would have to be revised, indeed many might vanish as we pull in more members at cheaper rates.

Also I consider that we do need to look at our hall hire charges with a view to making them more competitive in today's austerity environment. Money is tight, so the more folk we can attract to our premises to spend cash at the bar, the more financially viable we will become. An empty hall is a drain on our resources. With cheaper hire rates, we can make it a profitable entity. We must not look upon social members as poor relations. We need to lure many more of these social members to our bar of public opinion where they can drink cheaper than at any other local public house and in more pleasant surroundings and better company.

We need to fully exploit every means of revenue we can to put the club on a firm financial footing with the prospect of a decent future against the current constant decline.

This golf club has many fine assets that we need to better utilise. Rather than getting bogged down in interminable discussions about membership categories and the like, we should:

1, Shamelessly promote our competitive visitor charges of nine holes for a tenner and 18 holes for only £15 midweek, equivalent to about 83p a hole.

2, Boast that we are a nine-hole course ideal for time-starved players.

3. Police the fairways properly by acquiring an electric buggy and having members regularly patrol the course as marshals at busy times, especially on sunny Sunday afternoons, to get bandits to pay their dues.

4, Stress that we are situated in urban north-east London and merely a short drive away for the hundreds of keen golfers I see regularly on local driving ranges; even just a 30-minute car journey from a Canary Wharf full of stressed-out bankers.

5, Cheap golf plus cheap beer should be our slogan as we emphasise the 25% beer discount for green-fee payers.

6, Bang the drum for the club so that, certainly in the London boroughs of Redbridge and Waltham Forest, it is the natural choice for visiting golfers as it has such a high profile.

7, Slash subscription fees to £699 for all adult categories of membership, the equivalent of £13.45 a week or a mere 10 litres of petrol.

Brand awareness is of vital importance and we need to plaster our premises with the slogans mentioned above for there is no point in hiding our lights under a bushel. "Seven-day membership for £13.45 a week" would put rival club offers to shame. Brash boastfulness should be our motto.

We need to think the unthinkable. It is people who change the world. By acting collectively and with determination, we can rescue this golf club from its downward spiral and restore its reputation as the well-patronised "jewel in the forest".

There is no alternative.

Mashie Niblick, 2013 captain

Cometh the hour, cometh the maniac, Niblick later cynically remarked. Having truly nailed his colours to the mast, Niblick expected a whirlwind of objections to his ideas. He got nothing, not a peep from committee members for some days. He came across the club president, the secretary, his newly-minted vice-captain and all remained as silent as the grave, as if Niblick had committed the worst golfing sin imaginable, something that decent folk could not let go past their lips. There was just one individual, one of his regular playing partners, who later acknowledged that he had read the captain's long epistle and would be responding to it in due course but without committing himself to either support or oppose the ideas.

Meantime, the world ticked on and the rain eased up allowing the course to be played without golfers wearing Wellington boots like most of the course dog walkers. For Niblick, it was business as usual. His first two strikes in the March Medal hooked into the port-side woods, never to be found in the jungle of undergrowth. A further five balls vanished into the forest or beneath the carpet of leaves therein and so the world's worst golf captain yet again finished bottom of the pile, though he shared that dubious honour with four other members scoring a pathetic 22 stableford points.

A few days later, having been given a dozen newish balls by a sympathiser, Niblick got round the two circuits of the course and shed just one lost ball in the seniors' medal. A decided improvement on that front, though not much of a one on the scoring level where he amassed 24 points. And since the seniors never broadcast all the returns, Niblick just assumed that he was down again with the dead men for he was certainly a country mile adrift of one of his playing partners, Nick Rowe, whose steady and almost faultless round brought him a winning 40 point score. Now Rowe averred that he had played a lot more golf since his retirement a year ago and that had resulted in his handicap dropping from 12 down to eight. The logic sounded good until Niblick acknowledged that he too had played a lot more golf since his retirement 10 years ago, but his game had gone steadily downhill. His handicap had taken the exact opposite course increasing from 25 to 27 in tandem with his abysmal play.

Then suddenly, Mike Jones, the new competition secretary, produced a seniors' medal results list out of the blue and to his utter astonishment, Niblick found himself four places above the bottom man, although only two points better off. Was this the stirrings of a revival? Niblick shook his head for he well knew that one swallow never emptied a pint beer glass.

Meantime, there was yet another presentation to be made, this time to the former president and current secretary Peter Willett for his services to the club. Eight former captains and Niblick gathered in the clubhouse as Roy Webb, the president, presented Peter with a round gimbal clock on the day the the club launched its new range of beers from Greene King. The ales went down a treat, even though there were not swathes of members fighting to get to the bar as there should have been.

Niblick recalled how, during the reign of Captain Hugh Williams, he reckoned that there were around 10 Captain's friendly matches against other local clubs home and away, so he inquired of the secretary what was the form for this year's friendlies. A mere four in toto and three of them at home. The only real club match was against Whitewebbs, Niblick's favourite outing, but the away fixture coincided with Niblick's Spanish golfing jaunt, which was already booked and paid for.

Why the paucity of fixtures, two of them being against societies who had no home course to play? Clubs we normally have played against—Chingford, Theydon Bois and Royal Epping—had dropped out because they had had difficulty in raising a team, said Peter Willett. But the seniors' section still played them. West Essex and Chigwell had never been remotely interested in playing against us, remarked Willett. Niblick knew why. These posh 18-hole courses considered themselves a cut above playing against a measly nine-holer even though it had been going decades before they got their courses built. Snooty Chigwell, snooty West Essex, opined Niblick.

Around a week after he lit the fuse under his radical golf proposals, Niblick got his first real reaction in an email from the club treasurer, Mike Smith. He wrote: "I do not agree with absolutely everything you say but I do agree with the vast majority.

"I do hope you can encourage the Promotions and Marketing Committee to persuade the main Committee to take on the points about which you have written. Your enthusiasm and drive will be a big factor in getting us there and make your year as Captain a year of great contribution and worthwhile change."

At last, Niblick had some support. He was beginning to think that the rest of the management committee to whom the email had gone really considered him a nutcase and his proposals were the outpourings of a madman. No matter, he would pursue them vigorously until he got his way. Every car advertisement he sees, quotes £199 a month or only £359 a month without ever mentioning the price, except in tiny print which you need a magnifying glass to read. "7 day golf for only £13.45 a week" is pitched on the same lines. It is an absolute steal, according to the Captain. If that did not draw in more members, then a pole dancer was the final solution.

Meantime, the retirement of head greenkeeper Stuart Runciman loomed. Mind you, said Niblick, the "head greenkeeper" label was something of a misnomer as there was only one assistant, Steve Thorogood, who would take over. While Stuart could occasionally be an awkward cuss, Niblick had always got on well with him and decided to interview him with a view to writing articles for two local newspapers. Eventually, after bald-headed Stuart returned to work after a brief illness, Niblick collared him in the clubhouse and prised a decent tale out of the reticent man.

His mother had pushed him into art college when she recognised his latent artistic ability and Stuart prospered there gaining two travel bursaries from the Royal Society of Arts to travel to the USA and to Turkey and Persia. While staying with an Italian-American family in California who were friendly with Rocky Marciano, Stuart travelled with them to wave off the boxer when he boarded a light plane from San Mateo to Des Moines, Iowa, in 1969. Thus Stuart was one of the last people to see Marciano alive as his plane crashed killing the world's only undefeated heavyweight boxing champion, the pilot and another passenger. It is amazing what talking to other folk reveals about their past, said Niblick. "I once urinated in the next stall to Prime Minister Edward Heath at the old Press Club in Salisbury Court off Fleet Street", Niblick noted as if trying to back up the statement.

There was also a strong hint to Niblick that once he had finished his stint as captain, there would be a job awaiting him as press officer for the Essex Golf Union. The newly-minted EGU president, John Peters, announced this to Niblick and a handful of other members at breakfast in the clubhouse on a wet Saturday morning. Peters had been mightily impressed by the coverage Niblick had garnered both in the local newspapers and in the latest edition of the Essex Golfer magazine, which Peters had just picked up in the clubhouse. If a press officer job became vacant, would Niblick be interested in the role, Peters asked. Niblick made no comment. Without anyone knowing about it, Niblick hoped to be promoting the account of his captain's life in book form next year, not assiduously collecting golf scores from numerous competitions. But this was something he needed to keep to himself—and to his amenuensis—for he well knew that people would act differently towards him if they knew that he was confiding his opinions and views of fellow members to his scribe.

The dreaded March management committee meeting arrived and the fireworks that Niblick was expecting never ignited. Once the committee had agreed that it was not prepared to sit back and let the club slowly slide into oblivion, the positives began to emerge. With grateful support from the treasurer, members took aboard the proposal for cutting membership fees back to £699 annually, especially when secretary Peter Willett said that if we retained the current members, pulling in another 26 members would put the club in the same financial position as it is now with much higher fees. The finance committee will investigate ways of implementing this plan.

Another of Niblick's proposals, the one for a course marshal touring the fairways to catch green-fee bilkers, was warmly accepted years after constantly being shelved when Terry Insole and Niblick together pushed vainly for it. Something that Niblick had not considered was a suggestion from one member that when not being used for course marshal work, the electric buggy could be hired out to members. This was an idea that had come of age. The club needs to garner more funds before launching into buying a second-hand buggy, of which there are hundreds about.

That day, Niblick had got back an acceptable design for the club banner and he would be going ahead and ordering it. Other publicity ideas were being carefully appraised.

All in all, Niblick was happy with the outcome, although it was the club's dire situation that had forced this action. Cometh the hour, cometh the maniac, he repeated to himself.

It gave him pleasure to contemplate the retirement of the club's head greenkeeper, Stuart Runciman on his 65th birthday. Now the greenkeeper was someone who could not hold his beer—two pints and he's kissing everyone around him. Yet he was effectively the club's mascot as he had been in post longer than most golfers had been members. This is what Niblick wrote about him for a March article, most of which appeared in the Essex Golfer magazine:

After a glorious 43-year fresh air working life, Stuart Runciman has retired as head greenkeeper at the golf club, wrote Niblick.

Although he was trained as an artist, he thrived on the outdoor life. When Stuart answered a newspaper advertisement in 1970 for the job of assistant greenkeeper, the then head greenkeeper, Ernie Downey told the successful applicant: "Keep your nose clean, lad, and you'll have a job for life". The pair struck up a good relationship and Downey's words have proved true.

Class demarcation was much more prevalent in the 1970s than it is now. Stuart had to address all members, who were then mostly businessmen or members of professions and their wives, as Mister or Missus. They in turn addressed Stuart by his surname. "I felt something of an underling," he said. The gulf in status was plainly apparent especially on the day when Stuart told the incredulous club president, L.G. Jeffery, that Stuart's own grandfather, C.W. Jeffery (Royal Epping Forest GC captain in 1938) was the president's cousin. The club had around 400 members at that time and a waiting list of golfers wanting to join.

Since then, relations between the workers and the members have improved enormously; Stuart gets invited to club events, especially social ones run by the ladies' section, and is an honorary member of the club.

Born in 1948, Stuart favoured the outdoor life and worked on a farm for a year after leaving school. But his mother, who realised that her son was a talented artist, insisted that he should take up an academic life. So he went to art college.

One of his prized RSA bursaries took him to America, which is how he came to be one of the last people to see former world heavyweight champion Rocky Marciano alive. Stuart's other bursary took him to Turkey and Persia. He started his working life as a freelance artist, but found the going tough and decided he needed a steady job with a steady income. That is how he came to the club, much to the displeasure of his mother, who considered that he was wasting his artistic talent. It took her ten years to get over his snubbing of her advice.

Yet he put his talent to good use in 1990 when the golf club celebrated its centenary. In its glossy commemorative centenary brochure, Stuart drew remarkable caricatures of 22 "characters" at the club—including himself. At one point, though, he had to smartly redraw one member's image to remove the cigarette from his mouth as the man's wife firmly believed that her husband never smoked. Most of the characters he drew then are now dead.

Stuart loved being out in the open. When he started work as an assistant greenkeeper, the golf course was in much worse shape than it is now. The rough was cut back only once a year and big piles of grass were left in the high summer for a local farmer to collect to feed his horses. In the dry summer of 1976, there were frequent fires on the course, with members returning to the clubhouse in blackened shoes. "We thought that the course would never be the same again, but nature eventually prevailed", said Stuart. The club got off lightly during the 1987 storms, though heavy rain turning parts of the course into marshland in 2012 and early 2013 was the worst water damage Stuart has ever seen.

Labour needs also changed drastically over the years. When he started, it was a much more physical job with all mowing on greens and tees done by hand. Things changed in the early 1990s when ride-on mowers started being used. The cows that occasionally invaded the course, causing chains to be placed around the greens— "they could devastate a green with their hooves"—vanished about the same time when Mad Cow Disease was rampant.

Stuart took over as head greenkeeper in 1980. Despite the fact that he has never taken up the sport, he is almost a fixture at the club because he has been there longer than most of the current membership. Club Captain Mashie Niblick remarked: "Stuart's a cheery soul always looking on the bright side of life. He has been a huge asset to the golf club for decades."

John Peters, twice club captain and current President of the Essex Golf Union, said: "When we have had vandalism on the course, Stuart has been known to spend his own time on his hands and knees lovingly restoring our greens to their excellent standard.

"Stuart has always been proud of his work and the course, as amply illustrated by the high standard of preparation for the various Pro-Am's and County events that we have hosted over the years.

"He has always been popular with the ladies' section, but does upset them when he waters the greens in the middle of their competitions."

Stuart is succeeded as head greenkeeper by his own long-time assistant Steve Thorogood. He plans to wind down gently by helping Steve out a couple of days a week.

*   *   *

Stuart's tale casts a fascinating light on the stark gulf between what we might call the "nouveau riche" at that time and the "hoi polloi" looked down upon as the serving classes. At least the club eventually dispensed with its artisan section of poor relations, who did work on the course and could play only at certain times for modest fees, and made them all five-day members after World War II. There still are a few golf clubs in this enlightened day and age with artisan sections. Outlaw the lot of them, said Niblick.

Glum weather continued through March forcing the postponement of the seniors' match at Chigwell. Niblick complained vociferously when it was re-arranged for a date in June when the Captain's friendly away to Whitewebbs was scheduled. Niblick had already tried to change the date of the Whitewebbs visit as he would be away in a part of the world where rain or snow was not a daily occurrence, i.e. Spain. But in any case, a club with as small a membership as this one would be hard pressed to field two teams on a midweek day. And after all, Whitewebbs was the only away friendly in the year-long Captain's calendar.

Next up was the annual dinner of the Society of Essex Golf Captains at Orsett. Seven former Woodford captains as well as Niblick travelled by minibus to this fancy dinner-jacket-and-bow-tie affair where the wine flowed freely, the beef Wellington was delicious and the speeches humdrum. There must have been 400 there, Niblick reckoned, including a bunch in red jackets resembling the toastmasters. These it turned out were the representatives of Royal Epping Forest GC, the only club in the union with a royal appellation and thus scarlet dinner jackets. As he surveyed the multitude of golfing penguins plus the aberrant scarlet species, he wondered why none of them, or for that matter none of the 4,000 or so annual captains across Britain, had recorded their year for posterity as far as he knew, which left the field open for Niblick; he might not be able to chip but he could jolly well write quips.

While squelch golf was still the order of the day in March, Niblick had a remarkable experience on some dry ground while walking off the last green after a Friday swindle competition over nine holes. There in front of him and his partner were two green woodpeckers performing a mating ritual. Niblick and John Walker stood transfixed to the spot as these two lovebirds faced each other constantly swinging their heads and beaks and oblivious to the watchers for what seemed an age.

Occasionally their beaks would touch almost in the form of a kiss, and then one would spread its feathers behind and on the ground in provocative display. Eventually, after all this to-ing and fro-ing, one woodpecker flew off. "Cockteaser" remarked Niblick to his companion.

Good Friday was set as the day for presentations to John Peters, twice former captain and now Essex Golf Union President, and Stuart Runciman. All that had been requested of Niblick was that he should wear his captain's blazer and tie for the presentations. Niblick took his camera up to record the event, only to be told five minutes ahead of the presentations that he was to present a wine decanter to Stuart and deliver a speech.

So, without any preparation, he had to entertain about 70 members and friends with an account of Stuart's life, drawing extensively on the articles he had compiled for local papers and which they deigned to use. When Niblick thought his speech had lasted long enough, he inquired where the decanter was. It was still outside the clubhouse, so Niblick had to waffle on until it arrived. Then the man he had deputed to take the pictures said that the camera was not working. "Switch the bloody thing on," Niblick retorted and the pictures were taken.

Since just about all the other speeches were read from notes, Niblick had to acknowledge that he was becoming a master of the extempore delivery. He had done so at the 54th Society dinner and now at this event. Clearly it went down well because John Peters raved about it and Stuart Runciman told Niblick that he was the finest club captain that Stuart had come across in 43 years at the club. And Niblick reckoned that he had by this time hardly got his feet under the Captain's table.

It was common knowledge that the finances of the club were in an unhealthy state. Just how unhealthy, indeed critical, the situation was, emerged when treasurer Michael Smith dropped his bombshell in an email to management committee members. The club was £27,000 in the red, the worst situation it had ever been in, according to Mike.

Drastic measures would need to be taken to avoid the club going down the drain like the rain that had ruined last summer and was shaping up to do a repeat performance in 2013. With membership diminishing year on year, the club relied on green fees more than ever. There had been precious few of them last year because of the rain and there had been even fewer, proportionately, in the first quarter of this year, with many other local golf clubs boarding the same sinking vessel. Niblick's fear that the club was heading to the knacker's yard had suddenly turned from being a possibility to being a stark probability with disastrous consequences.

An emergency meeting of seven members of the management committee was called. There was ranting, there was raving, there was swearing as the embattled seven sought ways to conjure up money or, at the very least, cut back on spending. Not a lot was achieved, remarked Niblick, who chaired the contentious meeting. He had asked all present to jot down the ideas they had so that these could briefly be discussed and assessed on a scale of one to ten in their potential efficacy.

Getting rid of Sky TV was a popular notion. Games between far-flung Swansea and Sunderland, for example, drew hardly any viewers; it was only the games featuring West Ham, Tottenham or Arsenal that brought in the punters. The purchase of an electric buggy with which to pursue green-fee bilkers also won support, as did an idea for 5-year or 10-year membership categories to bring in more funds.

The really popular ideas that attracted the most support were for Gift Aid donations to be attached to membership fees, to increase the rent in a cottage owned by the club as well as turning the downstairs area of this cottage, now used as an office, into a self-contained studio flat, although this would cost the club money converting it when the pocket was empty. It was agreed to ask one member who had loaned the club cash to buy the cottage to defer re-payment of the next £5,000 tranche of his £15,000 investment, and to investigate getting a new bar computer to enable the club to set up various discount schemes much more easily than it could do at present.

There was precious little in the way of cutting expenditure or galvanising more income from the course if the weather did not turn for the better but continued in its remorseless dank and damp state. Then the club secretary pulled his rabbit out of the hat. He would approach a wealthy club member for the loan of £50,000 at around 4.5 per cent interest to tide the club over its current problems and allow the cottage office to be rejigged as a studio flat, thus enhancing the income the club got from it.

Now Niblick was somewhat critical of handing over too much financial power to one individual, but what was the alternative—purgatory? Reluctantly he went along with this idea, though one committee member could not stomach the shilly-shallying. Mark Bonham announced within days that he had had his fill of prevarication and would no longer attend the monthly meetings of the management committee, though he would continue to perform tasks associated with the greens committee. This was a substantial blow, though Mark did wear his heart on his sleeve and was loud in his condemnation of what he considered obfuscation. He was, remarked Niblick, perhaps a touch petulant when he did not get his own way. It takes one to know one.

After the secretary approached the club benefactor, who instantly agreed to defer the £5,000 he was owed, this man showed some remarkable business acumen in suggesting that the club should provide Sunday

36

lunches to all comers, as is the set-up at many golf clubs in Florida. The snag was membership, for the club would have to get around the problem of making all these mealtime visitors temporary club members. When the Sunday lunch deal had been tried solely among the members, it had not paid off, but extending the offer to all and sundry might well succeed, provided the club could sort out the membership snag.

There were more suggestions from the benefactor, some rather good and others with which Niblick disagreed. But the benefactor was showing initiative, which is to be commended, said Niblick. Yet Mark Bonham, who had publicly announced his decision to boycott management committee meetings, turned turtle and suddenly appeared at the next one, taking the chair when Niblick was stuck in an almighty traffic jam at the Blackwall Tunnel heading north from south London. Niblick got to the meeting half an hour late and after listening to Mark pursue his vendetta against one particular individual, Niblick was able to use his casting vote to save that individual's bacon.

Niblick issued a heartfelt plea from the Captain to all members urging them to maintain a £100 balance on the swipe cards which give them a discount on bar drinks. The message, printed in red, went up on all club notice boards and on tables in the dining area. It had modest success in giving the club a financial cushion, but there were a fair few reprobates who objected vehemently to the plea.

All about and around there were tales of financial distress at clubs, mainly due to last year's and this year's abysmal weather. At Whitewebbs, a great bunch of lads who play over the Whitewebbs Park council course in Enfield and have their own clubhouse, golfers said they were now down to 80 members and the night before Niblick visited with his own club's seniors, there was a break-in at the clubhouse. And so tight were finances at Royal Epping Forest GC at Chingford, that they went against tradition and did not invite neighbouring club captains to their 125th anniversary dinner. Poor Niblick was expecting an invitation after John Peters, the head golfing honcho in Essex, indicated that he (Peters) had been invited and expected Niblick to be invited as well. Niblick got no invitation and when discreet inquiries were made, the Royal Epping Forest hierarchy said no outside invitations—bar the Peters one—were being made, on financial grounds. Pity they did not tell other captains this for Niblick, for one, said he would have been prepared to have footed the bill for himself and his lady had any decent approach been made. It had not.

Members of the ladies' section gather around Mashie Niblick on Captain's Day

Then brighter and warmer weather arrived. Green fee income went up as promotions and publicity committee chief John Walker got to grips with producing a new leaflet extolling the club's facilities and charges. Niblick wrote some words welcoming visitors to the tough course which was no parkland ramble—a jibe at some other local courses where a slice just puts you on the next fairway rather than deep into the woods. The club was hiding its lights under a bushell, maintained Niblick. We need to whack people in the face with £7.70 a week golf for a year in the intermediate membership category. Boast about it, don't bury it under Special Offer lines, he thundered. When you go to buy a new car, the vendors laud their £199 a month offers only telling you what the actual cost of the car is in tiny print which you need a magnifying glass to read, he claimed. Niblick had already taken photographs of youngsters in the bar to indicate that this was not just a haven for old fogeys.

Meantime, Niblick's driving suddenly improved, but his putting let him down badly. In the Easter Eggs competition, he finished 16th out of 19 with 27 stableford points, the most points he had amassed in months. Nevertheless one of his partners, "Little" John Beecroft, whom Niblick described in a newspaper report as a promising novice, actually fulfilled that promise when he finished first on 46 points off his maximum 28 handicap. A strapping six-footer, he achieved this after taking up the game only a year before, whereas Niblick was a veteran of 60 golfing years. So Niblick wrote up the achievement in the local press. "Brilliant Beecroft" ran one headline. That's good enough for two free pints of Ruddles ale, Niblick opined.

The next day, Niblick sent John Beecroft and several of his golfing mates an email stating that there were too many Johns in the club and from henceforth he would be known as Brilliant rather than John. This nomenclature was taken up with alacrity and Niblick reckoned that the powerful long-hitter quite liked the new nickname. It reminded Niblick of a fancy headline he had once written. An Indian cook at a West Midlands school had been sacked for preparing curries that were too hot for the children. The Telegraph reported the case and the subsequent claim of the man when he took the school to an industrial tribunal. The delayed verdict went against the cook and Niblick was given the one-paragraph story to edit and stick a headline on. The clever headline was "Vindaloser". And while it provoked smiles that night in the office and no doubt next day among the readers when it appeared in the paper, Niblick had to acknowledge that the poor cook would be stuck with that moniker for life. Likewise Brilliant Beecroft.

It was rather rich, said Niblick, that when the foul wet weather appertained, he was the subject of playful banter when he stuck cycle clips around his trousers to prevent them getting caked in mud—"on yer bike" was the most popular jibe. And yet a quarter of the way into the year, folk were seeing sense. "That cycle clips routine is a rather decent idea" became the belief of several members who were averse to wearing the poncy plus two or plus fours and the club rules barred players from putting their trouser bottoms inside their socks. There was no mention of cycle clips, so, not for the first time, Niblick was ahead of the pack.

Next came the retirement of greenkeeper Stuart Runciman. Knowing the lad well over the years, Niblick had interviewed him for reports in the local papers and also in the Essex Golfer magazine. Norman Head, who runs the magazine, was extremely keen on the story and got Niblick to pare it back a bit in order to fill a whole page. With Stuart being a trained artist Niblick even put up the headline for the article: "An artist of the greensward".

At the subsequent presentation to Stuart, Niblick was sitting there in his pomp of Captain's jacket and tie and languidly inquired from fellow officials who was to make the presentation. "You", they chorussed. Somebody might have told me, said Niblick as he looked around with five minutes of preparation before John Peters, the Essex Union president strode up to accept a gift from the club. Peters, Roy Webb, club president, as well as the retiring head greenkeeper all had prepared speeches which they proceeded to read from sheets of paper. As mentioned previously, it was only Niblick who had to do the business extempore. A touch shambolic, he felt, but his audience seemed to revel in the unpredictability of events and gave the Captain and the greenkeeper prolonged applause.

Scotland beckoned. Now Mashie Niblick visits the cradle of golf at least once a year lured by malt whisky and the fact that his brother lives there and has been a member for years of the world's 13th oldest golf club,

Scotscraig, founded in 1817 and barely 10 miles from St Andrews. It is Niblick's contention that every self-respecting captain should visit Scotland during his term of office not just to kiss the turf at St Andrews but actually to play and experience the true tests of the game, whether it be on the Old Course at St Andrews or the marooned island course in the River Tay at Perth.

Scotscraig is, according to Niblick, a true exemplar of the Scottish golfing tradition. On his many visits there, Niblick has been made to feel something special in the clubhouse, but not on the heather, gorse and tree-filled links with a deep burn affecting three of the holes. This course has soundly shafted Niblick on his every visit. This time, playing with his brother and then changing partners every six holes, Niblick managed to lose on every hole, whether he was partnering his brother or the steady locals Graham Wallace and Gerry McCluskie. Niblick admired their play on the fairways but was even more impressed by the alacrity with which the rounds of drinks came up later on; he had barely got two mouthfuls down of the Belhaven bitter before another round came up. Niblick was hard pressed to fund a round because of the swiftness of the other lads in approaching the bar.

Of the numerous St Andrews courses, the one Niblick favours is the Castle course on the cliffs at the other side of the compact town simply because he once sank many dodgy putts on its undulating greens. There is also an institution at St Andrews that Niblick extols to the skies—the Seafood Restaurant next to the Golf Museum. On many of his recent visits to Scotland, Niblick has eaten at lunchtime in the glass box dining room overlooking the sea because it is cheaper then than at night. But on this brief visit, it was not feasible to lunch there so Niblick and the Captain's Lady together with his brother and sister-in-law booked a table for what Niblick described as the finest seafood dishes he had ever eaten. Washed down with Marlborough Sauvignon Blanc in a nod to the New Zealand origins of the Captain's Lady, it was not a cheapskate affair by any means; indeed it was one of the most expensive fish dinners the Captain had ever paid for. But it was worth it; it is not often that Niblick praises stunning food, but in this case the meal was absolutely incredible.

At the Grant Arms hotel at Grantown-on-Spey, Highland, while attending the 32nd gathering of Scotch Perspectives, a single malt whisky convention invented in Dundee by his brother and two university mates, Niblick came across the most incredible true golf tale he had ever heard in his life. It involved Derek Bramwell, of Hastings, East Sussex, a long-time member of the Beauport Park Golf Club, St Leonards-on-Sea, and a boozing friend of the Captain. It happened like this:

During the 1990s, Derek was playing some of those honesty-box courses in the West of Scotland, which are unmanned and where you place the fiver green-fee in an envelope, write your name and the date on the envelope and then post it in the honesty-box.

On the fifth hole, Derek drove off from the tee only to see his ball land in a river running across the fairway. Muttering various expletives, he walked to the river bank in an attempt to see his ball. Then, out from the waves in Excalibur fashion emerged a black hand clutching a golf ball. A head appeared and the frogman took off his mask. "Is this yours?" inquired the water nymph handing the ball to the astonished Derek. It was. Then the frogman explained that he was employed by the golf club to trawl the river bed for golf balls. As he was about to shift a pile into a bag, he heard a plop and saw Derek's ball heading towards him. So the frogmen caught the ball, surfaced and returned it to its rightful owner.

Now you could not write that true story in a novel, because folk would not believe it, Niblick told Derek. "But," said Niblick, "I could think of a fair number of folk who would have turned and fled as soon as the black hand emerged from the waters, even one or two that would have dropped dead on the spot".

This amazing revelation came after Niblick had retailed to Derek another astonishing true story told to him again by one of the participants at the Scotch Perspectives whisky event. It has nothing whatever to do with golf but is a fascinating tale all the same and bears recounting. Decades ago, a spruce young lady called Liz was driving from her Aberdeen home to visit her mother in Norfolk. On the switchback A68 in Borders country, she was stuck behind another car for mile after mile. Eventually the chap in the car ahead of her motioned to go into an approaching hostelry. Thinking that he was probably a salesman and that there was no chance of her being raped in broad daylight, Liz followed my leader into the car park. Once they had got a drink and began talking, they discovered that both were doctors and quite enjoyed each other's company. Shortly after, they married. Now in retirement, Mick and Liz McClennon live outside Lincoln. As Niblick later told some of the ladies at his own club: "There is a book in that, recounting the strange circumstances in which couples have met." It will not be penned by the maverick Niblick, that is for sure, but there was a subsequent sidebar to this, though again not a golfing story, but illustrative of the oddities in Niblick's life.

Heading south from Scotland along that notorious A68—sometimes wider these days than it once was—Niblick was looking for somewhere to stay in the vicinity of Haydon Bridge, Northumberland. His companion read out a list of possible places, one of which was the Barrasford Arms hotel at the tiny village of Barrasford. "I had my first honeymoon there 53 years and one month ago," said the Captain. "After the church wedding at Harton and the meal at the reception, my first wife and I left South Shields by train, changed at Newcastle-upon-Tyne and continued by rail to Hexham, where we then caught a local bus to Barrasford, near Hadrian's Wall. It was a fairly normal journey then when few people owned cars; today with rural bus services in decline, you would probably need to get a taxi from Hexham," Niblick told his companion.

At first reluctant, eventually Niblick threw caution to the winds and signed in for two nights at the hotel. "I was last here 53 years and one month ago," Niblick told the young receptionist. "April the second, 1960 to be precise". Word smartly went around the hotel and when they sat down for dinner in what was not the proper old dining room, chef Tony Binks, owner of the place since 2006, hove to and detailed the changes he had made to the stone building. The room set aside for diners was originally the lounge; the dining room that Niblick remembered was now the breakfast room. The trout hatchery just down the road had long gone. But the food was a lot better; chef Tony and his team do a fine breakfast with local ingredients and the hotel is deservedly famous locally for its dinner menus. This is no plug, but you read it here first . . .

Back in the golfing world, the club secretary came up with a bright wheeze to cut membership rates to £300 for the seven months remaining of the year in an effort to bring in more cash. This was eagerly accepted by the management committee, who pared the sum down to £299, a better deal than was on offer at any rival clubs.

The snag was that the deal was not being promoted properly. On the club's website, it was called "an incredible offer you cannot refuse" and then the details were buried among a mass of other information. Niblick got annoyed to put it mildly. "We need to shout it from the rooftops", he opined. "We need it in giant red letters at the top of the website's home page," he ranted. Apparently that could not be done, but in the end Niblick did manage to get the "£299 GOLF" message as the first notice you see when accessing the website. Small adverts were also placed in local papers. Promoted assiduously, Niblick reckoned that this deal could bring in another 50 members; after all, it was merely the price of the latest fancy driver with every bell and whisle imaginable.

Always keen to exploit the talents of members, Niblick applauded one new member, Neil Robinson who had joined the club after moving into the area. When he bought his house, Neil found that the estate agent gave him a welcome pack of various goodies. Could not the golf club offer a free two-ball round to newcomers via vouchers in the estate agents' welcome packs? He put this idea to 2012 captain Mark Bonham, who took it up with alacrity.

Of all the clubs he has played against in friendly matches, be they for captains or seniors, Niblick rates Whitewebbs GC of Enfield, the most entertaining. With a great bunch of lads as members and usually a delectable beef pie meal after the matches, these home and away games are Niblick's highlights of the year.

Niblick especially requested her best beef pie from caterer Gill Templeman for the home match, but what he had not reckoned with was the astonishing support that Kelvin Crouch, the Whitewebbs captain, brought along with him—his wife. Now this is the woman who, when Niblick asked for Kelvin's number on his last visit to Whitewebbs, no-one could supply it, but they could supply his wife Victoria's phone number. "You must be a stunner," Niblick told her when he rang.

Niblick was introduced to Vicky as soon as he reached the bar for the Captain's friendly. But according to Kelvin, she was Doris. That was the name he had dubbed her and that was the name to which this slim blonde dressed all in red and with red boots resembling Little Red Riding Hood answered as she accompanied Kelvin and his playing partner Hazel around the course.

Once she announced to Niblick, his playing partner Michel Jones and her own team that she would give a kiss to anyone scoring a birdie, Niblick was galvanised into action. On the fourth he chipped in off the green for a birdie—and a kiss. After he managed yet another birdie, he inquired of Doris whether net birdies counted for a kiss. They did and Niblick racked up two more net birdies to the one birdie by husband Kelvin. Then came the crucial question: what would Doris do for an eagle? She was non-committal. And for a hole-in-one? That was left to conjecture. A mighty hitter and an accomplished player, Kelvin drove the green on two longish holes, but he and Hazel lost the match by one hole, though Niblick claimed a famous victory of four kisses to Kelvin's one.

Then he wanted to know how much Kelvin would charge to rent out his wife as a cheerleader as she had lifted Niblick's game enormously. But no, Doris was Kelvin's prize asset.

When later reflecting upon the match, Niblick rated it the most enjoyable and oddly entertaining round that he had ever played. And it was all down to the folk involved. It is people that make life so fantastic, he acknowledged.

As ever in golf as in life, events change perceptions. Just when Niblick thought that the club was making modest progress in its attempts to attract more members and hence more cash, the club professional, Adam Baker, surprisingly resigned. The poor summer of 2012 and similar problems in 2013 had hit his income from giving lessons and getting a cut from the green-fees paid to the club, he told Niblick, allied to the fact that he was unhappy with the contract with the club that he signed as part of his retainer. It is the old story that wet weather deters golfers, maybe not so much the club players who have to compete in competitions on specific dates, but certainly those paying green fees. And it was green fees that were crucial to the club's survival and clearly to Adam's as well.

Now this posed a major dilemma for Niblick. He had championed Adam's cause at many committee meetings; indeed he said point-blank that he did not want to be captain of a golf club without a professional. That, he felt, would turn the club into a Mickey Mouse establishment, all bravado and no substance. Now he faced that prospect at the end of June. So what would he do now?

Here was the club on the brink of turning itself around. The huge banner had at last been brought into play on the forecourt, the website had been improved to push the £299 golfing offer, promotional advertisements had been drawn up to place in local newspapers and now came this spanner in the works.

Once the news emerged, Mark Bonham rushed to attempt to change the face of the club by suggesting moving the secretary into the pro's shop and making the secretary's current office the place for collecting green fees. Niblick was miffed. He sat down and penned the following missive to members of the management committee:

"In his euphoria at claiming his scalp, Mark Bonham has jumped the gun. I have not been told of what circumstances will pertain in the future in regard to Adam Baker and until the management committee hears that, no action whatsoever can be contemplated. It is the management committee that decides, not Mark Bonham, though his views will be given due weight.

"Personally, my view is that the club should contemplate employing an assistant professional to replace Adam, a youngster with verve and initiative. They are around, for other clubs have benefitted from their vigour and enterprising ways. It is well known that I consider that a golf club without a professional is like a headless chicken and I would not want to contemplate the club approaching its 125th anniversary in 2015 without a professional because then it would become the laughing stock of the Essex Golf Union, just as Royal Epping has become over its recent parsimonious arrangements for its 125th anniversary dinner.

"That is my own view and other management committee members will have differing opinions. But it is, I emphasise, the role of the management committee, not Mark Bonham unilaterally, to decide on the future of the club. In the end, the club is bigger than all of us."

The next thing was that the fancy 8ft banner proudly installed on the club forecourt broke. Instead of rustling in the wind while proclaiming the club's home, it suddenly collapsed like a drunk broaching the pub's exit door and hitting fresh air. Dishevelled and demeaned, it looked a forlorn sight on the club's forecourt. Measures were taken to complain to the manufacturers, Essex Flags of Ongar, who took up the complaint and promised to repair it within days.

As Niblick said to the Captain's Lady: these things are omens. Niblick recalled his father, a police inspector, remarking that everything came in threes. If one miner at Kirkby-in-Ashfield stuck his head in a gas oven—before the days of natural gas—to top himself, he would be followed in the next fortnight by two other gas suicides in the area. It was the way of the world.

So what disaster was heading Niblick's way? All he could think of was Captain's Prize Day on June the 8th. Up until the day before, fine weather was forecast. But on Niblick's big day, the Saturday, he was banking on the worst: he feared a snowstorm or some similar mishap.

It was nowhere near as bad as he thought: the third mishap was "Brilliant" Beecroft attempting to usurp the role of the management committee in organising a Twitter feed extolling the club and the course. This was not official, said Niblick. While he applauded folk—especially youngsters—getting involved in club affairs, they had to follow the official line and be endorsed by the club management. Although a popular lad, "Brilliant" had no authority, therefore his offer was untenable until sanctioned by the management committee. Brilliant claimed that no-one had objected by email to his proposal, so he was going ahead with it. It will be entirely unofficial asserted Niblick, who stated under his breath that he hoped that it might persuade a few folk to join the club.

On perusing the new promotional leaflet put out by John Walker, Niblick suddenly realised that while his epistle appeared on the leaflet, his name was nowhere to be seen on the website. Even the seniors' skipper, Dr Alex Lyons, got an honourable mention on the website, but there was nothing, not even a mention of Niblick's name on it.

When Niblick had accessed other golfing websites, he noticed that there was usually a prize photograph of the incumbent captain allied to a chunk of propaganda lauding his club and course. Now Niblick is not a man for self-aggrandisment; he prefers to hide his light under a bushel. But this was different: on the club's website, nobody knew him outside of the membership. Something had to be done. Then he looked up the Theydon Bois golf club website only to discover that his pal, Captain Michael Foster, was similarly ignored. Ah, perhaps nothing needed to be done as notoriety came with its own problems.

The kissing fields: The remarkable Doris with her husband Kelvin Crouch, Captain of Whitewebbs

As Captain's Prize Day—the highlight of his year—loomed, Niblick suddenly realised that the "Brilliant" Twitter business was a mere bagatelle; what really narked him was the fact that thesportshq, an outfit recommended by a previous captain, looked intent on letting Niblick down over the personalised golf balls he had ordered. Given that delivery was announced as 3-5 working days with an extra day added for the printing of the message, Niblick expected them to arrive at least three days before the big event.

When he received no notification that they were on their way, he rang up the firm to be promised that they would be there by Friday. By Thursday, there was still no despatch notification, so he rang again to be told by an operative named Joe that they would not get to the club in time. "Get me your line manager," Nibkick demanded. Will Mottram, the line manager, apologised for the firm being inundated with orders. "Well, my order will be cancelled if they do not arrive in time", said Niblick. Where there's a Will there's a way. Will said he would try to expedite the order and maybe get the balls to the golf club on Saturday.

Niblick had planned to give each Captain's Prize entrant a golf ball, a bottle of still water and a bar of chocolate. If the golf ball had to be presented after the players finished their round, then Niblick would accept that as the second best choice. Otherwise, thesportshq would be damned.

But the firm pulled out their finger thanks to Will. He later rang Niblick to say that the personalised balls would arrive the next day—and they did to great relief all around. As a result, Niblick wrote to Mottram's managing director (with a copy to Will) praising the initiative of his staff member.

Given fine weather, Captain's Day goes with a swing. Last year's skipper, Mark Bonham, supplied a list of the food he had provided, while Terry Insole, the 2004 captain and Niblick's side-kick, advised on the evening entertainment and effectively booked the performers and Peter Willett made prize-list suggestions and organised the movement of trestle tables from the clubhouse to a spot behind the ninth green where Tom Steed set up his gazebo. Things might not have gone as smoothly as Niblick had hoped, but everything was coming together on the big day.

While it was not the perfect summer's day, it was good enough: early cloud then sunshine and a stiff breeze and dry all day. Ever the resourceful eccentric, Niblick greeted every three ball to the tee with a loud blast on his hunting horn; so loud indeed, that it woke neighbours, among them the sleep-deprived golfer Anna Maris, who, after the second horn blast shouted angrily to her husband: "It's that bloody Niblick with his hunting horn".

Unaware of causing offence yet unperturbed had he known, Niblick went on to lecture each team of three musketeers on the stableford format, the nearest the pin prize on the "over the pond" ninth hole and the arrangements for the evening prize-giving, buffet and entertainment. "No show, no prize": That, said Niblick, was written in tablets of stone.

After offloading the beer, wine, soft drinks and food at the gazebo behind the ninth green, it was a day for Niblick to bask in the Captain's glory. He came to like being the Grand Panjandrum, proffering a tip here and taking a compliment there. And all the while, others, in particular the Captain's Lady and her helpmate Lynne Wade, were doing the donkey-work, churning out sandwiches for all and sundry. But Mashie had to acknowledge that having skivvies to tend to his every need was a pleasant experience. He could easily slip into the Grand Panjandrum role, though he was sure that he would soon tire of it. Maybe he could manage a Prince of Wales role for a month before endless treats of caviar became as boring as beef dripping on wholemeal bread.

So far as Niblick was concerned, minor mishaps were overcome and the day ended gloriously with a brilliant buffet provided by Gill the caterer plus music for listening as well as music for karaoke during the evening. The "no show—no prize" was invoked when the winner, Rob Ellis, failed to show up for the prize-giving, so the first prize of £70-worth of club-badged clothing went to Aiden Steed, who clocked 38 points to finish one behind Ellis. However, Ellis's name will be the one to go up on the honours board in the club. Young Ellis, a bearded brewery representative, later told the captain that he had had a prior engagement at a charity event with his wife at the Leyton Orient football club.

The next day, Niblick sat down to write accounts of the Captain's Day event for two local newspapers. Later on, he discovered that the Recorder's quite decent coverage of the event under a three-column photograph (also supplied by Niblick) failed totally to mention the Captain's name on his big day of the year. There he was in the photograph described simply as the Captain. The local Guardian managed to mangle the report somewhat, but at least had the Captain's name with their two-column image.

Then, just before the whip-night lads' trip to Spain came that third blow that Niblick had been fearing: his sidekick Terry Insole resigned from the club. Here was Niblick's big drinking mate, club captain in 2004 and a fund of advice, praise and damnation, indeed an ex-boxer who was Niblick's bar stool sparring partner, chucking in the towel while still on his feet. It did not make sense, but there was no time to question the pugilist before the lads left for Spain.

The younger generation of golfers, Chris Miller, Phil Gauci and Ben Rooney, line up with the aged skipper on Captain's Day

The 8-day jaunt to the Costa del Sol was the most bizarre Niblick had experienced in the last decade. There were exploding golf balls, fake watches tournaments, a knife incident, a tooth extraction, serial boozing and, most astonishing of all, a win for the Captain, a joint win admittedly, but the first time ever he had picked up any cash.

There were 16 in the party, mainly members of the Friday night whip gang, together with a couple of renegades who had left the club for pastures new and two expatriates from Thailand. Serial joker Dan Guinebault and his pal William Kleyn, a mobile phone entrepreneur, had enjoyed a previous jaunt and now made it one of their summer fixtures, admittedly combining the trip from Bangkok with a visit to relatives in England. It was the camaraderie and crackpot fun that they enjoyed; praise indeed.

Yet the outing started badly, with their easyJet flight from Luton stuck on the aircraft apron for three hours due to a strike by French air traffic controllers. Eventually when they took off, Niblick laughingly suggested that the Airbus plane should empty its bilges on some French airport that they were overflying to express their displeasure.

There was one huge bonus: the "thong of shame" was now history. In 2012, someone forgot to bring it. Now "we're all too old for it" explained one regular. In many ways this was annoying, according to Mashie. The tradition for years had been that the man who finished last in each competition had to disrobe and don this mankini to make a dash down the Torremolinos beach to the sea and back while being derided by beach babes and his own mates. Niblick had had close shaves every year, usually escaping because one member of the group had overslept and to oversleep and miss the outing qualified you for wearing the thong. Mind you, there were enough exhibitionists then and now who would volunteer to don the thong at the drop of a martini.

Before the golf on four courses began, everyone put in 100 euros to the kitty to cover prizes on each golfing day as well as an overall winner reward. Niblick was not confident as he reckoned to lose nine balls a round as was the case in previous years; balls down ravines, balls in bushes and in particular, balls in water as the Costa del Sol golf course designers seem to specialise in Spanish water torture.

So it was with a heavy heart that he set off on the first day on the La Quinta course at Marbella. And yet he hit a birdie three on the first hole: decent drive, chip on to the green and a single putt leading fellow players to wonder if this was the new Niblick emerging from past abject failures to the promised land of largesse. The question did not linger long in their minds as the Captain proceeded to lose balls in the numerous water hazards as usual. On a fine golf course, Niblick managed to muster 13 stableford points off his so-called 20 handicap over the outward half and then blew up on the second nine to total 18 points overall, an immensely respectable score according to Niblick's lights.

As he has done so often in the past, burly cabbie Martin Cox peaked early and took the day's prize. After that it was downhill all the way for Niblick's loud-snoring room-mate.

Bangkok Billy had had toothache even before leaving Thailand, where he had been told by medics, that their tablets would sort things out. They did not. So on the way back from Marbella to Torremolinos, the coach driver stopped off at a dental surgery and Bill, having lost the plot on the course, lost a tooth as well. His golfing pals quite happily occupied seats in the nearby Di Vino bar and sank beer and tapas as Bill supped pain killers. He was a changed man when he emerged from the torture chamber.

The form on these trips is to dump golf gear back at the hotel—the first hotel in Torremolinos if you are travelling east, but the last hotel in the resort if you are travelling west; i.e. it is next to the stream that divides Torremolinos from Benalmadena. Perhaps after a freshening shower, the lads then congregate at the Los Marengos beach bar to begin marathon boozing sessions.

When you sit on a beach bench under a parasol, you are constantly pestered by Oriental female masseuses and black lookee-lookee salespersons selling fake watches, flashing lights, dodgy designer sunglasses and the like, which is why Mashie Niblick prefers a bar stool inside. There is usually a whip going both inside and outside. These days Niblick does not have the stamina of his younger mates who regularly drink on, often at the McGuinness Irish bar, until 3am or even 6am if there is no golf scheduled for the next day. Niblick heads off to bed usually by midnight, otherwise he falls asleep in the bar. Old age is the cause, as it is for a few of the others in the party and in the rival group led by belligerent Ronnie Roast, though a fair few of Ronnie's tribe are non-golfers just out there for the sunshine and sangria.

Olleywally: Tony Olley tries out a lookee-lookee vendor's wig, glasses and fake watch on the Costa del Sol

The Cabopino course was a disaster zone for Niblick. As six balls went down the pan he racked up what he considered was a piss-poor score. It was the usual Captain Crap business. Even when, as so often had happened at his home course, he got within ten yards of the green, it took him another four lousy shots to hole the ball. Captain Crap indeed. Renegade Paul Swindells tamed the course to win by a mile off his handicap of one. He went up to +5 under the opaque domestic handicap system and that was the last we heard of him being in contention.

The lousy golf was spilling over into Niblick's private life. He ordered Wifi from the hotel for 30 euros a week only to find that it did not work and he packed in the order. So on his first day off Niblick set out on a mile walk on the seafront and behind it to find one of the internet shops he had used in years before. All gone. There were shops galore that had shut down, but the irony of this is that when Niblick returned to the Los Marengos beach bar, he discovered that it was a free Wifi zone. Sods' law in action yet again.

Now Aida Monica Mendez, who runs the bar with her partner Manuel Leon Gambero, took a shine to Niblick as he sat at the bar sorting out his iPad emails in between downing small glasses of beer and reading the online Telegraph. Two plates of tapas on the house came winging over to the Captain and when he called for the bill, it was a fair bit less than he anticipated. This is the life, he told some of Ronnie Roast's lads. "I much prefer the bar stool to the beach bench because sun-bathing is not my forte", he added. The barflies nodded in agreement.

As he sat there, Niblick could not fail to notice the tremendous endeavour by the various cooks employed in the bar. It was more than multi-tasking because they seemed to have half a dozen dishes on the go at any time and were totally in control of the food preparation for a couple of score of diners. It was a masterful performance. Niblick returned to the hotel for an afternoon siesta before heading off to the Parilla Argentina, an Angus steak bar in Benalmadena. It is a restaurant that he has visited on every Torremolinos trip because their Angus steak is so delicious. Invariably he has the same three-course meal: onion soup, the steak with a jacket potato, and fruit and cream washed down with a bottle of rioja tinto.

Others have joined him at the restaurant in the past, but none of the lads was interested this night as they preferred to watch television to see Britain's Justin Rose land the US Open title. The maverick that he is, Niblick is never phased by doing things on his own or for that matter being the deviant who goes against the grain.

You cannot forecast what daft ideas the lads will invent. On this trip it was to play golf wearing the huge and gaudy fake watches sold by the lookee-lookee men. One of these lads must have thought that he had struck a seam of gold when he flogged 16 of these fakes to the whip lads, including one for Niblick, even though the Captain was not there. The drunken ruling was that if you did not appear on the first tee on the morrow wearing one of these dodgy monstrosities, you got fined 10 euros under "local rules".

Niblick was as euphoric as Rose the next day when he became joint winner overall at the Rio Reale course. Indeed, had the Captain not played the wrong ball, and thus scored no points, he would have won it outright himself instead of sharing the prize with Tony Olley. The irony here was that seeing the Captain chip the ball decently on to the green, his playing partner Darrel James leapt out of their buggy, grabbed Niblick's putter and walked straight into an iron bench. When Niblick headed off to the buggy to tell his companion that the putter was not needed, he found Darrel writhing in pain on the ground. Niblick's first thought was that Darrel had been hit by a stray golf ball, a not unusual occurrence since all golf courses are missile firing ranges. Eventually Darrel recovered sufficiently to limp to the green with a large bruise beside his knee.

Anyway, the competition result was a tie on 26 points for the day's best stableford score between the Captain and Anthony Arthur Olley. There was also a tie on the scores for the back nine, so the winnings for both events were added together and then split between Mashie and Tony. The 115 euros winnings, Niblick's first ever on the Costa del Sol, more than covered his entry fees for the week. How did this come about?

It was, said Niblick, a flash in the pan. Mashie had long claimed that he was a rubbish golfer for 364 days in a year, then delivered one decent return. This was that day. He had metamorphosed in hours from Captain Crap to Captain Wonderful, all thanks, he reckoned, to that Angus fillet steak he ate the night before.

It certainly was a flash in the pan because the next day, on the glorious Torrequebrada course, Mashie was back to being Captain Crap. Shame that, because they always treat the lads well at this Benalmadena beauty, the closest decent course to Niblick's hotel. The whip mob play it every year without fail and are treated as honoured guests. Clare Egerton, their slim and feisty PR lass, welcomes the lads with open arms, giving them free coffee, free pencils and a free golf ball each and supplies prizes for the nearest to the pin on two shortish holes. The buggies are equipped with a satellite navigation screen, which she switches to yards from metres. The only thing lacking is a cool box on the buggy.

Lee Hellier was about to strike his first drive, when he was pulled back by some of the lads, ostensibly to have his photograph taken. Meanwhile Daniel Guinebault surreptitiously switched Lee's ball for another. As a crowd watched avidly, Lee smote that ball and was enveloped by a cloud of white powder; the exploding golf ball ruse had worked again. Lee later explained to Niblick: "I never noticed the ball switch. And anyway, I shut my eyes when I play a shot".

Despite his wearing a purple Torrequebrada golf shirt, Niblick's game started badly and continued in similar fashion. Though he lost only three balls against his usual nine on this majestic course, all Niblick could muster was a measly eight points over the 18 holes. In years gone by, this would have been a "thong of shame" defeat.

Beer comes to the rescue. You can either drink it to celebrate or drink it to drown your sorrows. Either way, you feel better, said Niblick. And with little Aida providing the lads with a modest beach barbecue, Mashie reckoned that the world was being put to rights.

Not in the Irish bar in the early hours, however, as a Spaniard drew a knife in an argument with an Englishman. One of the whip crew was about to go to the defence of his countryman when two plain-clothes policeman grabbed the Spaniard and his knife and the would-be assailant was marched off.

On their last full day, the whip lads and Ronnie Roast's mob arranged a late afternoon farewell lunch at Los Marengos. Argentine-born Aida provided lashings of food to the evident delight of the punters. It was an hilarious event with the Roast mob in particularly high spirits. As Ronnie had decreed that this was the last time he was organising the sunshine golfing jaunt, his whip crowd rivals had a modest collection to present the veteran Arsenal supporter with a memento. Carefully wrapped in a box and with a modest eulogy from Steve Parker, once opened by Ronnie, the gift turned out to be a sneide 10-euro Breitling watch when Ronnie claimed to have an original.

The room descended into laughter and catcalls with Ronnie's lads standing up to toast everyone from the Pope to the Queen to Ronnie himself.

Despite the evident drunkenness among the 40-odd boozers, there was a serious interlude when the lads made a cash presentation to Aida and her partner Manuel ahead of their planned marriage in September. The couple were genuinely touched.

During the whip crowd's eight days away, bar takings at the golf club plummeted by more than half . . .

Back at the ranch, reality dawned. There were just days before the professional would leave, the banner had broken yet again and Niblick's side-kick Terry Insole was adamant in his decision to end his membership of the Club. In a way, the last was the easiest problem to confront because nothing could convince Major Insole to change his mind.

He was fed up, he told Niblick, fed up with the management of the club, fed up with the attitude the management committee was taking, fed up with the clique he considered were ruining the club and browned off altogether. After delivering his resignation letter, he already felt better, said the major. He still planned to patronise the bar since his partner Cheryl Cook was still doing lunchtime stints serving beer and spirits to golfers.

Niblick felt that his pal was being foolhardy, but since they rarely played golf together but generally met up at the bar of public opinion, there was not going to be a lot changing in their relationship. The major told Niblick that he would have quit earlier in the year, but did not want to disrupt Niblick's Captain's Prize Day, an event that the major participated in.

Of much more moment was the disappearance of the professional as he collected the green fees and sold clothing and golf equipment from his shop. A stop-gap plan was instituted to get club members on to a roster to collect green fees. While this might work temporarily, said Niblick, it was no long-term solution. At least three professional golfers had indicated an interest in taking over the role of club professional, largely, guessed Niblick, because of the job's prestige since the club was founded in 1890 and was the second oldest club in the county union. Decisions on that front would have to await the July management committee meeting, though Niblick yet again made his feelings plain in stating to the committee that he considered a golf club without a professional to be a headless chicken.

Meantime, as green-fee income picked up modestly thanks to a sunny July, club secretary Peter Willett slashed the membership fee to £270 for the rest of the year, then finally down to £200 in a desperate effort to lure more golfers into the club. Just a handful joined. The earlier newspaper advertisement, while fine in its message, was placed on a general page full of other advertisements instead of being put, as it ought to have been, on the sports pages of the Recorder. Another wasted opportunity.

With the warmer weather, the seniors' section got into top gear with sunny visits to Theydon Bois, Epping Golf Course and Chigwell. All were pleasant affairs ending with good lunches washed down with lashings of bitter shandy, as Niblick had to drive back and found that he could sink a fair amount of shandy without contravening the drink-drive laws.

Even though Chigwell GC was a mere mile or so from where he lived, Niblick had last played there with the Daily Telegraph Golfing Society all of 40 years ago. He felt then that the Chigwell membership treated society golfers as inferior beings who were only allowed on the course under sufferance—and of course for their money. While Chigwell still manage to blackball prominent sportsmen applying for membership with a £1,500 joining fee, they seem to have shed that posh veneer so prevalent 40 years ago. It was this attitude that deterred Niblick from considering joining a club with a hilly 18-hole parkland course holding nowhere near the terrors of his own fairways.

Yet when he set out with his partner Anthony Weaver to compete against a tall and slim 77-year-old and his much younger partner, the Chigwell pair held total sway. Niblick acknowledged the old man's fine putting by labelling him the "master putter". It was a masterstroke on Niblick's part because at the drinks session after the match, the aged chap went around telling all and sundry that he had been described as the master putter and no-one anywhere had given him that moniker before. He was over the moon.

It was meeting a Chigwell member who was brought up in Doncaster, not far from Mansfield, that persuaded Niblick to do a loud rendition of "Slagheaps" for the benefit of members largely ignorant of its import. He did so after a rather pathetic series of jokes came from one of the home crowd and Niblick decided to liven up proceedings.

That was not the first master putter that Niblick had come across in his travels; there was Charlie King at Epping Golf Course. Notionally playing off 22, Charlie proceeded to carve up the noisy course where the M25 and M11 meet to stun his playing parters by returning a nett 52. He was devastating. Niblick could not even stand in Charlie's shadow.

Then Royal Epping Forest decided that they should properly celebrate their 125 years of existence with a beano weekend, which partly assuaged the snub Niblick felt when not invited to their 125th anniversary dinner dance. Captain John McKenna pushed the boat out with 18 holes of golf—interrupted by a gazebo "pit stop" near the ninth green for beer and biscuits—a buffet meal and then a prizegiving.

Niblick was paired with the garrulous Ian Timpson, Royal Epping president, Michael Foster, captain of Theydon Bois and architect of their recent successful push for more members, plus Peter Lawrence, vice-captain of Chingford GC standing in for their young captain, Mark Arkell. It was a lively game with poor Peter developing a wicked slice that, the more he tried to correct it, the worse it became. Michael was fairly steady, though he shanked the ball half a dozen times while Ian played on steadily and straight, amassing stableford points at just about every hole. As for Niblick, his golf was indifferent, though he did astonish his partners by scoring a birdie four at the tough tenth hole, a hole where he lost two balls only a couple of days before.

Without knowing it, Ian was, as Niblick averred, playing the Bill Deedes golfing method. Under this, as the former Cabinet minister and Telegraph editor told Niblick in the Waterfront bar on the Isle of Dogs in the 1990s, once your strength began diminishing, you punted the ball 100 yards at a time down the fairway. You rarely got into trouble and were on most greens in three or four shots. Then it was down to good putting.

Anyway, Ian notched 37 stableford points and won a wedge for his efforts. All three of the rest of the party got home with 25 points apiece. The glory of these outings is the camaraderie engendered by sportsmen with a shared interest in golf though from widely different backgrounds and professions, said Niblick. Indeed, Ian greeted Niblick when they first met in the bar with the words: "You are Robin Hood. I saw your picture in the paper yesterday." So that was a fortuitous business as Niblick had written a "Meet the Club" feature for the local Guardian weekly and managed to get printed with it, the image of him performing the Outlaw sketch with his Merry Men before his drive-in in 2012.

Captain McKenna had the nifty notion of getting special napkins printed with the message "REFGC Captains Day 2013 John McKenna". Sadly the apostrophe was missing from Captain's. Why is it that many golf clubs are so ignorant on grammatical matters? Theydon Bois seems to have abandoned apostrophes altogether and Niblick's own club is just as guilty despite Niblick highlighting their apostrophe foibles. All Niblick could reason was that if golf clubs whose members are among the brighter and better educated folk in society are that clueless, then what must be the case in clubs for the working classes?

The shock of the year came in late July. Niblick himself had drawn the pairings in the Minns Trophy when he managed randomly to get himself partnering Hugh Williams, the bearded Welshman who was the 2010 captain, and as dodgy a high handicap player as Niblick himself. In this greensome foursomes competition under handicap, most members rated the Niblick-Williams combination of beardies as 100-1 outsiders. How daft they were.

Niblick had his driving boots on and Williams called on his Welsh magic to ensure some stunning putting. A long Williams putt gave them a birdie on the first and then the pair never looked back, even though their opponent, club treasurer Mike Smith had to play on his own when his allocated partner Vince Thompson forgot to turn up. Thanks to Niblick's decent driving off the tees and Williams's deadly putting on the greens, the pair chalked up 47 points for their morning's effort. But being leader in the clubhouse was no guarantee of success as the afternoon competitors had everything going for them—hot sunshine and none of the rainstorms that the Met men had forecast, which both Williams and Niblick had banked on to ruin the afternoon players' cards.

And yet the bearded wonders prevailed, capturing the trophy by one point. It was, said Niblick, a gift from the golfing gods or, to put it bluntly, a fluke. Only a year before, Niblick had maintained that the only way he would get his name in gold letters on a club honours board was to become the Captain. With Hugh Williams and himself just nicking the cup, Niblick would see his name up there in gold on an honours board after the only proper win he had ever had in 60 years of playing; Williams already had his name in lights for his wins in two pairs competitions.

Now no-one alerted Niblick in the evening to his joint win and he even went on the Howdidido website to attempt to find out the result, but it was not there. So it was not until he reached the club the next day for a cooked breakfast and to pick up the trophy results and was accosted by Vice-captain Zekia Alsanjak and congratulated on the result, that he realised that he and Hugh were suddenly the flavours of the moment.

Once Niblick had written up details of the competition in reports for two local papers and sorted out some photographs, he went on the razzle. He listened in amazement to how others told of how easily their pairing could have won the trophy if this had not happened or that. A happy Niblick managed to stagger home without falling into bushes near the fire station and being rescued by fire-fighters, as was his wont after heavy boozing sessions.

These wins always come in threes, claimed his pal Paul Evans. "There was that win in Spain, and now this Minns Trophy success," remarked Evans. "What is it going to be next in this remarkable captain's year?"

Remarkable it certainly was for Niblick, but on the administrative side it was unremarkable. This was because of management committee waffle. Having spent his working life making decisions galore every night on a newspaper in Fleet Street and later on the far-flung Isle of Dogs, Niblick was more inclined to dictatorial powers than to the soul-searching and prevarication of democratic committee work. "You can't beat a bold man making a tough decision," said Niblick. "Then things get done."

They were not getting done at the club. A special sub-committee of three was selected to question the lads interested in taking over the professional's job, though with no guarantee that the club would even employ another professional. Fence-sitting, that's the role of committee members, said the Captain.

In order to get a better idea of how the club worked, Niblick volunteered to take over the role of bar boss. He had spent so much time propping up the bar that he might as well see how the other side worked. He once upon a time brewed his own beer, but this was a vastly different prospect to pulling pints with a handpump and working the swipecard till. But he never made it to the other side of the bar.

Then there was another aspect of life in which he was found wanting: running the pro's shop. The main task there was to collect green fees, so again he volunteered to step into the breach on a sunny Sunday morning, where, without much effort, he collected around £150 from players wanting to play nine or 18 holes. Cold drinks and snacks were also available and trolleys there to be hired out.

It didn't require much training to do this job, though Niblick admitted that he had taken a green fee on a credit card machine for the first time in his life. He also read most of what he fancied reading in the Sunday Telegraph while perched on a chair in the Secretary's office as well as various emails on his iPad. This was a cushy number, said Niblick. Even if he had made the odd foray out on to the course to catch any bandits attempting to play free, which is what the professional was supposed to do if not providing lessons at the time, it was a very easy number.

Of course as club captain, Niblick took on the role of salesman in trying to persuade these honest green-fee golfers to sign up for full 7-day membership for the last five months of the year for a measly £200, a stunning offer. He thought that perhaps three of the dozen or so golfers he spoke to might pursue the offer. There was a modicum of hope for Niblick at the end of his administrative stint when club secretary Peter Willett said a professional at a nearby club was interested in taking over the shop and putting one of his assistants in it to give lessons and collect the green fees. The club had managed for a month without a professional with an extra burden put on the secretary and those members who had volunteered to help out. Clearly using unpaid volunteers was a system that would not last long, so here was a possible solution.

The beginning of August brought hilarity galore to the membership when Niblick was featured as a contender in a competition for the worst-dressed golfer in the county golf union. There was Niblick sporting his Robin Hood garb together with a daft jester's hat on his head, a ukulele in one hand and (naturally) a glass of bitter in the other and the legendary Captain's name as the caption. Whereas all the other players featured in this golf magazine column clearly were in the business of swinging a club, Niblick looked to be swinging the lead. This came only a couple of days after he had been pictured with Hugh Williams in a local paper, both of them looking like upstanding sobersides. The contrast could not have been more poignant: Honest Mashie in one publication, daft Niblick in the other.

The fascinating Aida, a Torremolinos beach restaurateur, and her fiance Manuel salute the lads after they had a collection for the couple's imminent wedding

It was back in April that Niblick had the idea of going with his brother, Nick the Professor, on a "pilgrimage" to their Nottinghamshire golfing roots or a drive, as Nick lucidly put it, down memory lane. So Niblick then booked up outings at Sherwood Forest GC in Mansfield, Coxmoor GC at Sutton-in-Ashfield, Worksop GC at Manton, and finally, the place where it all began, the Notts GC at Hollinwell, Kirkby-in-Ashfield, where the brothers took up the sport after being employed as teenage caddies.

There, decades ago, Old Tom the caddymaster would loan them a set of clubs if they had no job and the lads would play the first three holes at the course, which brought them back to Old Tom's premises beside the pro's shop.

The brothers would cycle six miles from their home at Sutton-in-Ashfield on Saturdays and Sundays to carry members' bags around the course to earn five bob a round in old money.

In 1957, Mashie Niblick joined Coxmoor Golf Club, Sutton-in-Ashfield, as a student member for £1 a year subscription. Later on, his brother Nicholas James joined as a junior, but was not permitted to play in competitions until he was 15 years of age. Just a few weeks after he turned 15, young Nick captured the Easter Cup. Nick went on to win competitions at Coxmoor, Sherwood Forest and Worksop when he was a member at those clubs.

Indeed, when he got his handicap down to four, he was offered a job as an assistant professional at Lindrick GC, the championship course near Worksop, but he turned down the offer to pursue an academic career, becoming Professor of Visual Perception at Dundee University. He is a world authority on the subject and has written numerous books on psychology.

The Professor entered wholly into the spirit of things on this odd pilgrimage with the Captain, by bringing with him from Scotland a set of golf clubs that he bought at Coxmoor more than half a century ago. The clubs were purchased from Bill White's pro's shop at the Sutton club and the covers of the woods still bear the faint impression of "Coxmoor Golf Club". The Bobby Locke Personal irons cost the Professor the princely sum of £35 and the Ben Sayers woods seem miniscule in comparison to today's huge beasts. They also had leather grips, which are more slippery than today's composite ones. He loaded them in a 70-year-old leather golf bag given to him years ago by an uncle, Geoff Ostick, one-time captain of Retford Golf Club.

Before going out, Nick renewed his aquaintanceship with Alex Shepperson, once British boys' champion and now the Coxmoor president. Both went to Queen Elizabeth's Boys' Grammar School in Mansfield, though Alex is a good bit older than Nick, who is 71. Ordinary members at Coxmoor were delighted that the pair had returned to their old stamping ground and were particularly interested in the ancient clubs and bag. Indeed one chap proudly boasted that he was 82, had only one eye and was still playing golf. "My mates spot the ball for me," he explained. Niblick commended him for his resilience. He was a credit to the game.

Then, after posing for his picture to be taken beside the cockerel statue on a plinth, commemorating the Coxmoor centenary in 2013, the Professor embarked on a round of golf with his brother. Neither was prepared to reveal their scoring, though the figures did improve marginally over the four days of golf.

The Coxmoor club and the course have changed radically over the years; when the Retford-born brothers played there half a century ago, the layout was substantially different. The old clubhouse and the pro's shop run by the inimitable Bill White, whose bright golfing career was ruined by the war, were in front of the first hole, which ran down a steep-sided valley. The buildings have been demolished to be replaced by new quarters and the old first hole is now the 13th. There are also many more trees that have been planted in the intervening years.

"They have changed the whole character of the course by this wholesale tree planting," said the Professor. It used to be a moorland course as the name implies, he added, and was much better for it.

His brother concurred. "I recall whacking my ball into the heather and grass rough and having to kill off rabbits galore blinded by myxomatosis to put them out of their misery. It was a heathland course then; it no longer is," said Niblick.

Similar results from tree planting are apparent at the Sherwood Forest and Worksop clubs, two of the four courses where the brothers went on their nostalgic trip to their old golfing haunts.

The least changed of the courses they played was Hollinwell; it was still recognisable as the place where they lugged members' bags around 18 holes at weekends. Indeed in the 1950s and early 1960s most of the members then hired caddies—usually teenagers or miners wanting a day out in the fresh air—from Old Tom. Those golfers playing with golf bags on pull trolleys were labelled "cheapskates" by the caddies.

But in the subsequent decades, the use of caddies declined and then ended. When Capt Niblick inquired if he could hire a caddy for his round, he was told that none was available and had not been for years. The modern-day replacement, an electric buggy, could be hired. The Captain shunned this modern contrivance in favour of his own pull trolley, while his brother carried his own clubs over his shoulders as he did all those years ago and still does at his home course, Scotscraig, in Fife; Nick is also a member at St Andrews.

Inevitably, there have been changes at Hollinwell over the decades, but the Notts club has managed these remarkably well and is embarking on a programme to axe some of the trees and vegetation that have sprung up over the last 60 years.

"If I turn on the memory clock," said Capt Niblick, "I particularly remember the uphill 11th hole where we caddies stood in the rough halfway between the tee and the green to spot the members' tee shots. Then came the mountainous 12th followed by the valley downhill to the 'postage stamp' 13th green. They remain

With a 70-year-old leather bag and clubs more than 50 years old the Professor poses beside the plinth marking Coxmoor's 2013 centenary year

indelibly imprinted on my mind.

"Of course as menial hod carriers then, the clubhouse was totally out of bounds to us. This week was the first time I had crossed its portals since, as a current captain, I was given the courtesy of the course."

Both men wrote in the visitors' book lauding the Hollinwell course. The Professor wrote: "Having caddied here over 50 years ago, it was a delight to enjoy the course as a player. It should be noted, however, that the change of roles has mixed blessings—it is easier to watch poor shots than to play them. In our caddying days, Old Tom, the caddymaster, would encourage our participation in the caddies' competition (which I had the good fortune of winning once). The experience of caddying spurred me to play the game, which has occupied a large section of my spare time in the intervening decades. One of the joys of playing the course today was to note that it has retained its character and resisted the blandishments of 'course reconstruction'. The course is as recognisable today as it was five decades ago and is as difficult and testing. Long may it remain so!"

Golfers, Niblick noted, were among the friendliest folk around. At Sherwood Forest they were joined by a member, Peter, a consultant solicitor and decent 10-handicap player, who was able to show the brothers the pitfalls of a course so changed that they could barely recall the layout of 50 years ago.

Then at Worksop, 16-year-old Reece Samson showed the brothers how to tame the Manton course. Reece took up golf when he was just over 10 years old, has stuck at his last, now plays off a handicap of two and figures in the county under-18 team. Assisted by his ball-spotting grandfather Dennis, a retired Creswell Colliery miner, Reece managed to get around the course in par much to the chagrin of the Captain and the Professor, who was once Notts junior and then youths champion. Indeed Reece was so steady on the fairways that the only ball-spotting that Dennis did was to locate the brothers' dodgy shots.

The lad was gobsmacked when the Professor recalled the time he played at Worksop before the town bypass, which runs beside the course, was constructed. In Reece's short life, it had always been there and he could not imagine a time when it wasn't.

Reece's ambition is to become a professional golfer like the former Worksop member Lee Westwood. Aided by Worksop's Captain Keith Hearnshaw, the Professor was able eventually to locate a Worksop honours board where he was listed as the club's scratch champion in 1961 and 1963, years before young Westwood got a hat-trick of scratch prize wins.

While Nick was winning cups in west Notts, his brother was in Africa golfing in Northern Rhodesia (now called Zambia) while working as a journalist, before enjoying a 30-year career mainly as a news editor on The Daily Telegraph in London's Fleet Street and later on the Isle of Dogs. There he played top courses such as Wentworth and Walton Heath with the Press Golfing Society and later more mundane Home Counties venues in the Telegraph Golfing Society.

Both brothers rated their pilgrimage as a highly successful event. "It is not just some of the golf courses that have radically changed over the years," said Captain Niblick, "Mansfield is almost unrecognisable as the town we grew up in. There are retail parks and supermarkets everywhere where once there were factories.

"When we lived on Forest Avenue, only my mate Toz Osbourne's father had a car. Now cars are ubiquitous. The vast increase in traffic lights makes parts of Mansfield resemble Blackpool illuminations and the huge rise in traffic and new roads mean that the Coxmoor and Worksop courses in particular suffer from noise blight. In contrast rural Hollinwell is a haven of tranquillity with buzzards, sparrow hawks, a heron and a host of multi-coloured butterflies in evidence," Niblick remarked.

"Mansfield used to be known in my youth for its football team and for its beer. Happily, the Stags are back where they belong in the Football League, but it is an absolute scandal that Wolverhampton and Dudley Breweries (now called Marstons) shut down the Mansfield Brewery plant in Littleworth in 2002. That was a shameful decision by greedy brewery directors and their accomplices.

"Still there is always hope. Micro breweries are now taking up the cudgels as we found at Worksop Golf Club, where they sell the delightful Welbeck Abbey Ales, and at Hollinwell, where, appropriately, a Captain's tipple is available produced by the Pheasantry Brewery near Newark. Life is change, but not always for the worse."

For such an outing booked months ahead, the brothers were blessed with magical weather. Warned by the Professor of heavy rain on the Sunday in early August before their first game at Sherwood Forest the next day, Niblick brought along three pairs of golf shoes and three pairs of trousers assuming that they would get soaked daily and that they would have scant drying facilities in their motel.

Yet after completing 18 holes and showering, they walked back to the clubhouse lounge to see the rain tipping down. It had eased off by the time they left. The menu at this highly security-conscious club—missing the entrance, Niblick had driven in through the exit gates—was short but good as the club, right on the edge of town, is going through a process of clubhouse renovation.

After that narrow escape, it was plain sailing weather-wise, not excessively hot but neither cool. And no rain.

The bugbear at Sherwood Forest for Niblick was the heather and grass running about 70-100 yards from many tees. When he got caught in this stuff, it was generally three shots to get out. And the trouble for the Captain was that the more he thought about this gunge, the more he went into it. But that's golf; it is as much a mind game as it is a physical one. It is a commonplace that you don't let it get to you, that you shrug it off and forget it. Easier said than done, as the cynics say. It has happened often enough to Niblick and to many of his friends.

Niblick recalled his mate Major Terry Insole in 2005 hitting a lovely drive on the 15th on the Old Course at St Andrews, then fluffing his second shot whereupon his club was hurled further than the distance the ball travelled. His third angry shot went straight into the hole for an amazing birdie. After being harried earlier on by mardy-arsed stewards urging us to move on—"you're half a hole behind" was one ludicrous complaint—this one shot made the Major's day.

Meantime, Niblick bumbled along in his usual inept fashion. On one outing, he sank a 30ft uphill putt on the fifth at his home course for a bogey five, then was on the green for three on the difficult and long dog-leg sixth with a chance of nabbing a birdie, or at least a par. He five-putted the ball on the upturned saucer of a green. Five-putt Niblick became the laugh of the clubhouse.

Not a misogynist, he played with women for the first time in several years (apart from the odd time with his sister-in-law), when invited by the lady captain, Irene Dupree, for an outing with her pals. Irene and Niblick finished last. He also partnered Barbara Fitzpatrick—a far better player than Niblick on the day—in a Captain's friendly at Whitewebbs when the men ran short of players. They duly lost their match despite a valiant show by Barbara. Yet there was a marked improvement when Niblick partnered Zuby Skinner in the Harvest Classic invitation event for mixed teams of seniors and ladies; they finished third from last.

But this latter outing got Niblick turning over in his head thoughts that only a person with a dirty mind, like Niblick himself, might consider: the ambiguity of terms and phrases used in golf that have decided sexual connotations. For a start, there is the proposition by the lady golfer holding the flag to her male companion to "just pop it in". Then again there is the call from the distraught lady stuck in the rough to the male member—here we go again—to ensure that his balls are clean.

And ignoring that crass shout by loudmouthed Americans at events like the Ryder Cup— "in the hole, in the hole"—we English have a much more subtle attitude to cheering. "Don't get your knickers in a twist", Niblick said that he heard one golfer admonishing his decidedly heterosexual mate. Whether male or female, you have partners, just like couples living in sin, though perhaps in the 21st century that term is a little harsh so perhaps co-habiting would be better. Of course your partner might be high dependency (high handicap) or magically competent (low handicap) just like wives or concubines. Innuendo lurked behind any mention of bush, lip or kiss.

Now normally, there is a pattern to the golfing year. Fixtures are arranged well in advance so that the club can get a calendar printed with the dates of all the major (and minor) competitions listed. Effectively the weather rules the roost and can cause the postponement of matches though not usually the cancellation. It is when a club unilaterally changes fixture dates that the problems arise.

There is an agreed date for the playing of the Forest Cup, a competition between all the clubs who play on Corporation of London land in Epping Forest; it is the second Saturday in September. Well, the 2013 hosts, Royal Epping, changed the date to the first Saturday, much to the consternation of rival clubs and protests from some of them. Niblick's club had to change the date of the monthly medal and no doubt other contests were similarly displaced.

The 2012 Forest Cup holders, Theydon Bois, duly entered a named team but on the re-arranged day of the competition, not one of their members showed up at Chingford golf course. The course is across the road from Chingford Plain, where medieval kings had vassals round up deer and send them scurrying across to where the monarch sat in his hunting stand armed with a crossbow to pick off what animals he chose. With so many deer, the king could not miss.

Theydon could. They effectively got their calendar pants in a twist. Yet the show must go on. Go on it did with an outcome that surprised everyone for the club with the smallest membership led by the youngest captain, Mark Arkell, drove their way to glory. It was a close-run thing, but they beat their older brethren, Royal Epping, by just four points. Both clubs, plus Chingford Ladies, use the same municipal course, but efforts to merge them have always failed.

The event, at which Mashie Niblick showed up in his Captain's jacket and tie in order to cheer on his troops, showed yet again the camaraderie that golf competition engenders. He was greeted effusively by two members he had competed with before, and almost made to feel a member of that rival outfit. Other captains greeted him like a long-lost brother. Truly, said Niblick, this was the epitome of club golf where you become bosom friends with folk you have never encountered before.

Yet another crass bungle merely emphasised Niblick's general incompetence. Just after "Brilliant" Beecroft's wife, the art-loving Anna Maris, had got back from a trip to Germany, Niblick inquired where she was, as usually she accompanied her husband on his bar outings. "She's in Brazil", said Brilliant. "Bullshit," scoffed Niblick. "What you mean is that she's gone to the Brazil art gallery". A couple of days later, Niblick emailed Anna to say that he had managed to get a tiny picture of her and three mates having a pitstop rest on Lady Captain's Day into a local newspaper. "Don't forget to pick up a free copy of the paper when you leave the tube station this afternoon", he told her.

Niblick was stunned by Anna's swift reply. "I am just looking at Ipanema beach from my Rio hotel room," she wrote, "so I won't be picking up the paper at the tube station". And to rub salt into Niblick's bruised ego, she appended a picture of the glorious South American beach.

On to more weighty matters: there was a prospect of ending the interregnum of being without a professional. One chap, already the boss boy at a nearby club, suggested that he could take over the role and place one of his smart assistants in the shop to collect green fees, give lessons and sell golfing gear under his general direction. The club leapt at this proposal, met the pro and drew up an agreement which committee members hoped he would sign. While Niblick felt that there were already too many golf courses in his area, he just wondered how Surrey, with a smaller population, could support over 130 courses. It did not make sense.

Then the banner collapsed yet again. This large white sail announcing in red the home of the golf club has been plagued with what Niblick loosely termed erectile dysfunction problems, that is, its main member regularly collapsed. All it needed was a rain storm to undermine its stiffness. Yet, as Niblick remarked, he had passed garages with six banners on their forecourt that never went limp as did the club's promotional post.

With the club's annual dinner-dance only weeks away, Niblick was called upon to decide on the menu in consultation with Gill Templeman, the caterer. Now Niblick was used to ordering steaks for himself in restaurants, much to the displeasure once of his second wife, an Olympic runner who constantly condemned his failure to try new dishes, but Mashie was not used to ordering or even thinking about the food needs of others. Gill had not been altogether happy with lamb shanks she had prepared in 2012 and the club secretary had hinted to Mashie that fancy chicken might be a decent substitute. Niblick was appalled at this because chicken was a commonplace everyday dish and the 80 or so punters expected at the event, each coughing up £46 a head, deserved something special. But what?

Beef pie kept coming to mind as Gill made spectacular versions of this, but, as Niblick ruminated, this was also a commonplace because Niblick always requested Gill to serve it up at any of the meals after the Captain's Friendlies that he hosted. These plain dishes went down a treat with normal carnivores; Niblick could not care less about the vegetarians, the vegans and their strange ilk.

Gill solved his dilemma in one sentence: "How about fillet steak in a fancy red wine sauce?" she asked. Manna from heaven, that's what Niblick thought. As she had had so many compliments from Niblick for her meat pies, the Captain reckoned that she had probably read his mind. Anyway, fillet steak it was for the main course and the subsidiary starters and finishers were agreed without much discussion.

Yet there were only a few names up on the board listing the folk who had decided to attend the dinner-dance. Niblick thought he might boost the uptake. He had worked it out that a number of the lady members might well be attending on their own as their husbands or partners were uninterested while there were others who were widows or divorced. He wondered whether, if he announced that Captain Niblick, not known to be an ace on the dancefloor, would dance with all the unattached women, this might boost the attendance, or not.

He sounded out Anna Maris, a lady knowledgeable in these matters. Anna was horrified. The idea vanished from Niblick's head far quicker than it had gestated there.

With never a dull day, Niblick's next task was to pick his team for the annual Captain v Secretary when the two of them picked names alternately from the list of 40 members who had decided to play. When it came to selecting the pairs, Niblick, used to making instant decisions in Fleet Street, had his team settled inside a minute; the secretary took much longer, possibly because his team had won the match seven times out of the last eight and he was intent on maintaining that record. Anyway, the selections proved absorbing for the membership. And even though he had bought a stock of port as he was continually being called upon to top off this event or that with a bottle of port, the Captain was determined not to stick his hand in his pocket this time since the losing officer funded the winning team with wine—and that inevitable bottle of port—at the evening dinner.

The Professor smites a drive towards the distant clubhouse on the 18th hole at Hollinwell

While Friday the 13th was unlucky for some, for Niblick is was his bonanza day since the club that day had signed up a new pro. This lad—and he was a lad, as Niblick was three times older than him—at 25 was extremely young (plus point for Mashie) bearded (plus two points in Mashie's book) and a livewire familiar with the joys and perils of social networking on the internet (another two points in Niblick's estimation) so that he was at this juncture the ideal choice.

Kenny Banks had the right golfing background—he took up the game when he was seven or eight—the correct qualifications and had lately been mentored by Bradley Preston, head pro at Woolston Manor GC and the Top Golf Centre at Chigwell. Bradley is the head professional overseeing matters although Kenny is the man the world meets at the club. The only snag was that he would not start for a fortnight.

Anyway, after Bradley and Kenny had toured the pro's shop and decided on what to stock and where to place it, Niblick managed a brief session with the pair so that he could take their photographs and then took Kenny aside in the club lounge to find out a bit more about the lad's background. The Captain, the veteran of two wives followed by a string of mistresses, then offered the lad one piece of pertinent advice: "Never get married".

With that injunction ringing in his ears, young Kenny went off with Bradley in the slight drizzle to familiarise himself with the tough jungle course.

Niblick faced up to a formidable programme of golf matches involving an outing every other day. The punishment to his body began to build up and finally he succumbed to the inevitable; he bought an electric golf trolley. True it was used, it was cheap and it was basic. But on his first outing with it, he realised what a boon it was. He was able to stand upright and view the fairway with the motorised trolley in front of him instead of being bent almost double with his pull trolley behind and his eyes studying the ground rather than the green.

Niblick was one of those golfers who had always denigrated the electric-trolley lads, some of them even as young as 50. He had vowed to keep on pulling his two-wheel bag carrier almost until he dropped on the grounds that it would keep him fitter than the softies. His brother was prehistoric in this respect, still carting his full bag over his shoulder as he had done for more than 50 years.

It was after his third game inside four days that Niblick noted that the club was selling some equipment, clothing and this second-hand electric golf trolley. As his back was aching, he asked to borrow it for 18 holes to try it out. It worked a treat and so for a measly £45 Niblick acquired this electric trolley probably five or six years old and donated to the club by a wealthy member who had upgraded. A Hill Billy brand, it had two batteries and two chargers and just a small handle wheel to start it, stop it and accelerate or slow down. This was fine for Mashie as he had no time for satellite navigation, scopes and the like with which modern trolleys are equipped.

Occasionally he admonished colleagues on the course with the words: "You've got eyes, use them". How many golfers, he asked, were so accurate as to need to know whether the distance to the flag was 171 or 177 yards. Just getting the ball on to the green was the sole requirement in Niblick's opinion. But golfers are always the optimists, which is why golf magazines are chock full of glossy colour advertisements for this gadget or that. Clubs change quicker than women's fashion accessories. All you have to do, according to the golfing sage, is to wait a year for the new driver with "more power, more accuracy" to appear and then buy the previous year's model for a third of its original price when it then was extolled in advertisements as having unprecedented power and accuracy. A prize cynic is Niblick.

The sage invested a lot of endeavour into selecting his team for the fiercely-fought annual contest between the Captain and the Secretary. A week before the event, the two of them sat down to select their teams. Niblick paired stronger players with weaker ones and reckoned he had the perfect combination to halt a run of seven victories out of eight by the Secretary's lads.

It turned out to be a close-run thing, but Secretary Peter Willett cleverly outsmarted the Captain to run up his eighth success in nine years. It all hinged on the last match with the score at 4.5-4.5 points. Two of Niblick's men who had won prizes over the summer suddenly lost form and fell at the last hurdle by a massive 5&4.

Mind you the auguries were not good when Niblick went out with Hugh Williams to face the Secretary and his five-handicap partner Mark Deeming. Niblick was abysmal, playing arboreal golf, yet luck was with him when his drives ricocheted off the trees on to the fairway. Welshman Hugh kept them going with Niblick hanging vainly on to his coat-tails.

Deeming, though, had just had some putting lessons from a professional and was deadly on the green. The Captain and his mate were thrashed 5&4 and the galling thing for Niblick was the only decent shot he played was with the wrong ball that landed 10 ft from the pin on the Punch Bowl. But that's golf, he opined, you're up one day and down the next, though it does pay to mark your own ball clearly so that you can spot that it is yours even in thick grass.

Later when he moaned to the 2001 captain Chris Phillips that he must be the world's worst golf captain, Phillips responded: "Oh no, we do not just pick our captains for their golfing ability, but also for

Erectile dysfunction affects the club's hang-dog promotional banner, seen beside the sole ball-washer on the course

their character." That was an ambiguous remark in Niblick's books. Character could mean a person of substance, an honest and reliable individual. Or a character could be a deviant who wore odd socks, told loudmouth jokes and generally acted as if there were no social rules in life. Niblick reckoned that he was the latter character.

Not only did Niblick's plucky lads lose this prestigious competition for a cheapskate cup, but they had to buy the wine and port for the winners at the evening bangers-and-mash dinner. That is rubbing it in, said Mashie. Given three large sausages on each plate, one greedy Irishman toured the dining room begging spare sausages until he devoured 11, though this was a good bit short of the club record of 16 eaten by one ravenous member.

There had been a couple of afternoons during periods of drizzle when, as is usual, the promotional banner flopped. It was suffering from erectile dysfunction, said the Captain. Numerous attempts to stiffen its main member quickly failed. The tall banner became known as floppy Dick.

Incensed at this downfall, Niblick wrote a stiff email to the supplier's representative as follows:

DEAR GEORGIANA,

Yet again the banner that the Golf Club bought from you in good faith in May has collapsed. It has been back to your premises for repair but still is not fit for purpose. Every time it rains, this banner suffers from erectile dysfunction. Since you last repaired it a few weeks ago the rod has snapped or become disengaged three times and one of our members has attempted to repair it with tape. This has not worked and the banner is currently in a sagging position.

I drive past petrol stations galore to see their numerous banners standing up to the elements while ours, a vital promotional tool for the club, just wilts. I am disgusted by the standard of workmanship your company has provided and ask you to rectify this as soon as possible.

Yours etc.,
MASHIE NIBLICK, CAPTAIN

A couple of days later, a representative of the supplier telephoned the club and Niblick to say that he would be down next day to fix the banner on the premises. He was down, but it was in such a sorry and delapidated state that he took it away to the firm's headquarters at Ongar, Essex, saying that he would bring it back once it had been properly fixed. A Viagra moment, as one wag opined.

Off to Maldon Golf Club in Essex for a charity event, Niblick was meticulous in packing his bags. There was a full change of clothes, washing gear, bath towel and he even packed sunglasses in the hope that the sun might emerge some time in the afternoon; it did not. He shunned the electric trolley because he was going there and back in a mini-bus and took instead his pull trolley.

And yet in alighting at Maldon, he contrived innocently and accidentally to drop his bag with his golf shoes in it on the gangway. By the time he had found that his shoes were missing and searched the changing room and car park for the bag, the bus had sped off and the driver declined to answer the telephone when Mashie rang.

Captain Nigel Cook helped out by suggesting that Niblick try the shoes abandoned in the changing room, but all were too small for Mashie's size 10 feet. And the club did not have a shop for selling such items. Then St Peter came to the rescue. Maldon's Vice-captain Peter Hawkins nipped down to his car and retrieved a pair of white size 11 golf shoes that did the honours. Trust Niblick to land in such a scrape.

Maldon is a flat parkland course with bunkers, but few other problems. You can get away with zig-zag golf as Captain Cook did, so you don't lose many balls. What you do encounter on this isolated nine-hole course, though, is a yap dog. Based at some distant house, it barks incessantly on a Saturday afternoon. Maybe its owners are out shopping, but that dog needs restraining, possibly with a tight muzzle around its mouth. It barks more than a kennel-full of yap dogs and even at times drowns out the traffic passing over the Chelmer river bridge near by.

The Maldon club is small and old—though a year younger than Niblick's home course—and it has one thing Niblick has always desired, a captain's throne. 'Tis no humdrum, ordinary chair like the one at Mashie's club, but a carved masterpiece. Not that the club knew all that when they acquired it, for it then had a padded back. It was only when the padding was removed that the chair revealed its full glory. Now it bears the brass plate "Captain MGC". Niblick sat in it to contemplate the world and its golf balls. It made him feel a master of the universal fairway.

Now the reason for the Maldon trip was to compete for the David Webb Trophy, presented by the hero of that name who was a member of both Maldon and Niblick's home clubs before he succumbed to cancer in 2009 aged a mere 39. Niblick said that rarely had he seen such fortitude in an individual as David displayed. He treated the cancer that was gnawing away at his vitals as if it were a common cold. When most folk would have thrown in the towel, David battled on, even travelling with the "whip lads" to Spain for a golfing jaunt where he was the life and soul of the dinner parties they threw.

This was why the "whip lads" had no second thoughts about playing in the annual competition; they wanted to salute the man and his abiding memory. His dad, Roy Webb, announced after the tied match that £400 had been raised for the cancer unit at Barts hospital, City.

The celebrations went on long after all the Maldon members left their bar. Indeed when the mini-bus arrived back in London at the forest car park, Niblick accidentally picked up his trolley and his bags and set off for the first tee in pitch darkness before realising the error of his ways. A golfing pal helped him stuff his clubs into his shed locker, whereupon Niblick dumped his bags in the changing room while there was a raucous birthday party going on at the club and then staggered downhill on his way home without falling into the pathside bushes. However, the last time it happened, in 2009, when firemen rescued him, Niblick proudly boasted that the fish and chips he was carrying were still hot when the firemen presented him to his mistress at the house front doorstep. Trust Niblick to land in such a scrape.

By the time he had competed in the Captain v Secretary match, Niblick reckoned that he was suffering from golfing overload and set about drinking shandies rather than the Best Bitter he was used to. Next he had withdrawal symptoms, not over the ale but over a day without golf. Still, he reasoned, there was the Seniors'

Shield upcoming in a couple of days.

He was drawn to play with the automaton Tom Steed, a bearded low-handicapper with a penchant for decent play. So with Tom's undoubted steadiness allied to Niblick's stroke-a-hole allowance in the four-ball better ball stableford competition, they stood a fair chance.

They won it. This was not through any particular merits of Mashie's abject performance, though he did come in on about four holes to manage a half. No, Niblick rested on Tom's shoulders on all but the short last hole, where tall oaks bar the way to the green. Unexpectedly, Tom sliced his ball into bushes, while Niblick's tee shot bounced on the green and then took a wicked turn to the right. Tom was effectively out of it, so he cleverly advised his partner to get down in two and secure three stableford points.

Under no real pressure as he did not know his own team's score, never mind what others were doing, Niblick lazily chipped on to the green to within 3ft of the cup. Niblick then sank the putt without realising that it was his most crucial shot in the whole round. Just sinking that putt snatched them the Seniors' Shield. They amassed 44 points, but if that putt had not gone in, they would have tied on 43 points, but lost out on a count-back as the runners-up had a superior score on the back nine.

While that is the third cup that Niblick has won in the last four years, it has to be acknowleged that not one of these was earned on individual play. His first trophy, the Jack Craig Cup was won while partnering Andy Efreme and Tom Steed—that man again—in 2009, the Minns Trophy with Hugh Williams earlier in the year, and finally the Seniors' Shield. A coat-tailed clown some people called Niblick behind his back.

A proper Captain's Throne shown off by Captain Cook at Maldon Golf Club

In normal circumstances, a bottle of port would last Niblick five years. As a beer and malt whisky man, he sipped a modest glass of port occasionally at golf club dinners, but perhaps only at Christmas at home. Captaincy changed all that. There was the bottle of port he was expected to provide for this dinner and that plus the four or five for the club's annual dinner-dance.

He was buying so much of this fortified stuff that he considered becoming a port broker. Then came the Past Captains' Cup. Niblick was invited to play, but could not win the Cup because this was restricted to past captains and Niblick was the current holder of the office. Yet he was expected to supply the port for the gourmet dinner, which, naturally, he did.

Of course, Niblick finished last, mainly because he lost six balls on his round, three of them in successive shots. On the short ninth, he put his drive smack bang into the middle of the pond sited just yards from the tee. No question of a provisional, for that strike was a goner. His next tee shot went a little further, but still plopped desperately into the pond. Niblick was flabbergasted for it was more than a year ago when he last went into the pond. He gave up scoring on that hole and then on the 10th, smashed his drive into long grass on the port side of the fairway—that drink again—and never found it. Now that was some going, three lost balls in three strikes; it had never before happened to him, especially when only three days earlier he had managed to complete 18 holes using the same ball.

But there was some cheer for Niblick later on when he came across John Peters, President of the Essex Golf Union and twice a past club captain. "I was expecting to win the cup," said Peters. "But I have a record seven blobs on my card."

"Hang fire, Squire," responded Niblick as he pulled out his pathetic stableford card. He totted up his own blobs—a mere six; done down yet again.

The past captains, plus other skippers unable to play, treat themselves to a fancy dinner with fine wine—plus the Captain's port—as befits a gallery of heroes who have struggled each for a year to lead the club to the promised land which is always a distant chimera.

Niblick missed it all—the port as well. He had accepted an invitation to Chingford Golf Club's annual dinner-dance because during the whole of Niblick's captaincy, he had been able to take the Captain's Lady to only one other event and that in the previous November, when she had twisted her ankle and arrived at the event leaning on a walking stick, unable to dance. Ever the compassionate captain, Niblick reckoned she deserved a second outing, particularly as she had acted as his chauffeur at various unofficial events.

Having only a small clubhouse, Chingford chose to hold their dinner-dance at Theydon Bois Golf Club, way out in the countryside where deer roam and snakes slither. Fortunately for Niblick, a piece he had written together with a picture he had taken for the Essex Golfer magazine was published that weekend to the evident delight of Captain Mark Arkell of Chingford and his heavily pregnant wife Leeanne.

It was a lively affair. Niblick quickly realised how out of touch he was with modern times when a host of songs played by the disk jockey Niblick had never heard before. Suffering from aural torture, he marvelled at the current dancing fashions. These days you never needed to ask a lady for a dance as everyone shimmied by waving their arms about and getting their legs to do a jig. Quicksteps and waltzes, which Niblick was used to, were clearly infra dig.

Mind you, Niblick was quite chuffed to hear that his own dinner-dance had attracted 81 folk. As he was languidly reflecting on his popularity in the club, it quickly dawned on him that by inviting his three offspring and their partners plus his brother and sister-in-law, he personally was bumping up the attendance materially.

He ordered a case of port for the event and delivered it to the club secretary. Then he got down to writing his speech, mainly a summary of his amusing early golf experiences with a bit on cheating—not as expansively as he had spoken at the 54th Society earlier in the year—but with a passing mention of Charlie the Cheat as it reminded Niblick of a dead member of his club whom he declined to name. This tall former athlete got up to nefarious activities on the course only to wow the whole company at dinner with his immaculate joke telling. He was so good at recounting a yarn that he was forgiven for his petty ball-shifting in the rough.

After a swing around Hollinwell, one of the finest courses in the Midlands, the Professor and the Captain relax after lunch

The Club's dinner and dance, held near the end of the Captain's term in office, was one of the final highlights of Niblick's year. Some captains approach it with trepidation as the Captain is the centre of attention and has to make an important speech. None of these terrors plagued Niblick as he was confident making speeches and had his knocked off in an hour at least five days afore the event. Indeed, he even went so far as to suggest various lines that his son might pursue in the reply he would make toasting the golf club.

Niblick mixed humour and self-abnegation in his oration as any of his mates would have expected. And to top it all off, the Captain's Lady decided to bring along her violin to accompany the Gaffer when he made his inevitable rendition of "Slagheaps of my Youth", the first time ever it had had a musical accompaniment, but then the Captain's Lady had heard the poem recited innumerable times so she knew what was upcoming. Niblick abandoned the idea of launching the poem with a blast on his hunting horn.

Kenny Banks, the new professional face of golf at the club

On the Saturday morning of the event, Niblick went out early in the October medal with Brian Meggs, a staunch Leyton Orient supporter, but with a passing interest in the fortunes of Mansfield Town. Expecting rain after checking out the weather forecast, they went equipped to get soaked, yet found the weather fine, a fair few clouds but occasional sunshine. This was an augury for the whole day. There was Brian playing the best round of his life inspired by competing alongside the Club Captain. As Niblick later wrote in one of the local papers, Meggsy was an accountant well versed in juggling numbers. But the amazing numbers he totted up on his card were nothing like he had ever seen before.

He finished with a 61 nett off his 28 handicap, thus sweeping the board in division 2 of the medal. Ten shots way back in Brian's wake was the runner-up, Mitchell O'Brien. It turned out to be a costly affair for Meggsy as his handicap was cut by four strokes just a week ahead of his appearance in the Tigers, Foxes and Rabbits competition.

Niblick fared less well. After the opening nine holes he was on course to break 100 for the first time in a few years, but he blew up on the inward half even though he never lost a ball and this latter was an achievement in itself as he had lost six balls on his round in the Past Captains' Cup the week before. Brian also used the same ball on all 18 holes, though he did lose two provisional drives when he thought that his proper drive may not have been findable, but it was.

As Mashie Niblick strode back to the clubhouse with a card recording 109 strikes of the ball over 18 holes, fellow members greeted him with heavy faces and doom-laden comments such as "Oh it's the Captain's big day" or "Good luck tonight, skipper," implying that he might contract the collywobbles and thus dry up with fright and need all the luck going to keep his head above the parapet. But anyone close to Mashie knew that he was made of sterner stuff; the only time that he would wilt under pressure was in making a vital putt on the last green, but never at the bar of public opinion. His Fleet Street schooling had taught him to play the long game and not to worry about short-term rebuffs.

He got home, showered and put on his evening dress awaiting the arrival of his brother Nick the Professor and his wife, plus his own three offspring, Guy, Claire and Penny and their partners for a few pre-prandial glasses of wine as well as commemorative photographs of the family all together on a happy occasion rather than the inevitable grim funeral gatherings when a relative drops dead.

Once at the Wells Club where the dinner-dance was being held, Niblick came across an over-wrought caterer Gill Templeman, who had been allocated only one small corner in which to prepare a hot meal for 80 diners. She had had to lug the food back to the golf club to half cook it before returning to the Wells Club to finish it off. She was clearly at her wits' end and almost in tears. But Gill is a proper trouper and she stuck to her last to provide a delicious fillet steak in a mushroom and red wine sauce for the main dish of the evening.

At the Wells Club, the Captain and his Lady welcomed guests as they arrived and then, just before the guests sat down for their meal, Niblick and Ms Susanna Ferrar nipped outside the dining room before being formally announced as they marched in to Table 1 to applause from the diners. Then came the easy part, the saying of Grace by the Captain. Once the meal was over, President Roy Webb proposed the toast to the Queen and then Niblick got up to toast the guests. This was what he said:

"Welcome all of you to the Golf Club's annual dinner-dance, and a particularly warm welcome to the President of the Essex Golf Union, John Peters and his partner, to Captain John McKenna and his wife of Royal Epping Golf Club and his neighbour Captain Mark Arkell and his wife from Chingford Golf Club as well as the new face of professional golf at our club, Kenny Banks and his girlfriend.

"Welcome also to my three offspring, Guy, Claire and Penny and their partners plus my brother Nick and his wife. Additionally, I would like to salute Brian D'Arcy, of the Tower of London Golfing Society and his wife Peg who last week celebrated their 60th wedding anniversary.

"Most of you here are golfers or at the very least golf widows, so you have some notion of the fascination, indeed the passion, that the game exerts on players. It is a mirror image of life where there are regular ups and downs and yet some manage a rare consistency in their play, always being in the chase, or in my case, invariably being out of it.

"It is the perfect antidote to today's stressful existence. Golf keeps you fit, increases your longevity and adds a distinct social dimension to enhance your enjoyment of life whether at a quiz night, at the bar of public opinion, or at a dinner-dance such as this one.

"For me, who started his golfing existence as a caddy lugging clubs around a posh course outside Nottingham for five bob a round in old money, the game of golf taught me a lot about life. For one thing, I discovered that golfers are even bigger liars than fishermen. Another surprise was that there are more cheats in this game than footballers committing so-called professional fouls. I observed it all as a caddy: the player's deft flick of his shoe when no-one was looking, to improve his lie, the scraping away of leaves under which the ball is buried magically to shift it away from a tree root, and worst of all Charlie the Cheat who carried spare Dunlop 65 No 5 balls in his right hand pocket and had a large hole in his left-hand trouser pocket. Charlie indicated to me that when I found his ball in a difficult lie, I was to bend down to tie my shoelace and surreptitiously pocket it. I then gave Charlie a wink and he would wander off to find a decent lie, slip the new ball down his left trouser leg and cry "I've found it". Of course I was complicit in his cheating, but my reward was six bob a round from Charlie. He never entered competitions did Charlie but was a generous host to his playing partners at the bar. So he got away with it. As for me, I was happy with the extra bob well knowing that if I shopped Charlie my caddying days would be over. Take note also, that the first club I joined, Coxmoor at Sutton-in-Ashield charged me the princely sum of £1 for annual student membership.

"But talking of golfers who magically move balls without any apparent human intervention brings to mind one of our staunch members, a former athlete now sadly deceased. As everyone in the club knew, he was a dab hand at ball shifting but he was also an extraordinary raconteur. To hear him tell risque jokes was to listen to a master story-teller. So good was his delivery that in the end everyone forgot about those little kicks with his shoe which you were not supposed to see and forgave him for his trickery.

"When I took up this game, there were many fewer courses than there are now. While in Scotland it was the national game, played by rocket scientists and road sweepers—I met one such at my brother's home club, Scotscraig in Fife—in England it was, until about the 1970s, elitist and expensive. I recall an aged solicitor once remarking about 20 years ago to my father that in their day, there were only two players at Worksop`Golf Club with handicaps under five. "Now there's half a dozen, all plumbers, builders and electricians", he said in exasperation.

"The democratisation of the sport has had untold benefits in luring folk away from lazy television-viewing into a game so fascinating that they wonder how they existed before taking it up. It is perfect for footballers and cricketers whose knees have begun to creak because once they have had lessons and cracked the rudiments of the game, the handicap system puts them on a level playing field with their golfing peers.

"The problem today for us and for many other members' clubs are the peripatetic players who venture from course to course like wandering minstrels depending on which course has the better breakfast or free buggy offer. These are sunshine golfers without proper handicaps who need to realise the value of club membership in competitive play, in camaraderie and in co-operating to enhance their own and the golf club's standing.

"Our greatest challenge now and in the future is to revitalize the club by boosting its membership. It will not be easy, but we have already addressed the issue and are considering ways how to tackle it. You can all play a part by encouraging these itinerant golfers to join under our cheap trial membership schemes. We are all in this together, ladies and gentlemen members.

"Incidentally, this dinner-dance does not just happen out of the blue. It has to be organised, a venue selected, a menu chosen and all manner of other minor details settled. It needs dedicated volunteers to create this event. I salute all of them, and in particular Peter Willett, who has been untiring in his efforts to keep the club on an even keel in the interregnum when we were without a professional this summer.

"Ladies and gentlemen, before I ask you to raise your glasses to toast our guests, I will inflict one short poem on you. It is entitled 'Slagheaps of my Youth'. It was written by me in 1978 and refers to those giant pit tips around Mansfield which were my mountains as a child. It is a paen to a lost landscape and is traditionally recited every Christmas at a Daily Telegraph lunch for former staff. I know a few of you have heard it before and perhaps are cringing in your seats dreading the repeat rendition, but there are others to whom this poem will be a revelation."

Having previously tuned her violin, the fiddler on the hoof accompanied Niblick as he bellowed down the microphone. The outcome was unique; indeed the 2009 captain Mark Deeming was so overwhelmed he was left writhing in his seat unable to contain himself. The rest of Niblick's audience were more muted. Most knew that the Captain would launch into "Slagheaps" at the drop of a hat and never be deterred by walkouts or complaints. This was Niblick's signature tune for it set him apart from all the other golf club captains in the world. How many of them, he would ask, has ever written a poem never mind one so illuminating as "Slagheaps".

Once the tittering and twittering had died down, the Captain's son rose to respond with a toast on behalf of the guests. Guy remarked that he had never recalled Mashie Niblick ever giving his own son a lesson, or for that matter his two daughters. "Nevertheless, the fact that there were always golf clubs about in the garage, some admittedly with persimmon heads, enabled me more or less to get the hang of the game on the back lawn whacking plastic balls," he said.

"The one thing he has always complained about is losing balls. On his taster round before joining the golf club in the late 90s, he consistently outdrove all his three playing partners, but his aim was somewhat awry. He lost 12 balls on that outing. He has improved marginally; last week in the Past Captains' Cup, he lost only six, but three of those were in successive shots—two into the pond on the ninth and the third being his wayward drive into long grass on the 10th.

"He has frequently described himself as Captain Crap—and with good reason, according to his drinking mates—and yet, as I well know, he has the interests of the golf club at his heart. In his wildest nightmare, he never expected to be Captain of the club, but as usual, when the chips are down the tough get eating. As last man standing, he arrived hesitantly at the starting line, but was there when it mattered. He launched his captaincy with an outlandish Outlaw sketch with himself as Robin Hood riding a hobby horse on to the tee while blowing a hunting horn and aided by the "whip night" lads as the outrageously-clad Merry Men. Anyone who witnessed it, as I and my sisters did, will never forget this crackpot sketch, which outdid Monty Python. Inevitably there then came the downfall: a pathetic inaugural drive of 35 yards off the tee. But the captain then told me that the drive was a remarkable success. He hit the ball and remained standing: one member had placed a £1 sweep bet on the Captain falling off the tee . . ."

That was it. Dancing began immediately afterwards. Captain Niblick remarked to one of his friends that the Captain's Order of the Day was short and simple: Have fun. They did.

Despite various members informing Niblick that they had enjoyed his speech and the club secretary claiming it had been the best dinner-dance in years, Niblick shrugged off all compliments for he had a match upcoming, representing the seniors' captain's team against the seniors' secretary's lads. In particular it was a pairing between Niblick and Hugh Williams, a former bus conductor. Not only had these two bearded wonders captured the Minns Trophy a few weeks earlier as a duo, but they had form.

Niblick recalled playing, maybe a dozen years before, with Mick McShea against new member Hugh and his rugby and golfing mentor and fellow Welshman Julian Greatrex. Neither of the Welshmen had the honour on the tee until the 15th so battered were they.

In the Seniors' Cup, the boot was on the other foot. Conditions were grim. Thick morning fog ensured that any drive beyond 70 yards disappeared into the mist. Then once the fog began to clear, the rain came down persistently.

Not a morning for great scoring then, though it never is for Niblick; he could have the sun shining on a balmy day on a links course with a bikini-clad lass carrying his bag and shoot just ten over—ten over the hundred that is.

Niblick thought he stood a great chance as Hugh, whose game had improved over the years in parallel to Niblick's golfing decline, had to give away eight shots. After four holes, Niblick was four down. Ground staff had hollow-tined the greens a few days before so that every green was criss-crossed with straight-line spike marks.

This ruined Niblick's putting; it galvanised Hugh's. The bearded smoker sank putt after putt, reformed smoker Niblick missed putt after putt. Even when he had two for a win, Mashie succeeded in three-putting. This was masterful golf by Williams and miserable play by Niblick. Hugh triumphed by 5&4 thus helping the Secretary's team to lift the Cup.

But the major test was still to come: the Tigers, Foxes and Rabbits competition with Niblick naturally captaining the Bunnymen just a few weeks before he became the ex-skipper.

It was one of those classic golfing days where everything—bar Niblick's prowess on the fairways—was superb. The day began with a cooked breakfast at the club and continued with raucous banter between the Tigers team of low handicap players, the Foxes men with mid-range handicaps and of course, the Bunnymen, those bandits with high handicaps whom many claim deliberately do not put in score cards so that they can maintain the fiction that they cannot play well.

The teams of eight more or less selected themselves. The captain then drew the trios to play each other in a competition revived by Major Terry Insole during his 2004 captaincy when it looked like it was becoming moribund. Then competition secretary Michael Jones chucked a dry wood lump on the tinder box to ignite fierce protests from the Tigers. His new rule of the day was that everyone should play off their full handicaps—normally it would have been three-quarters of their handicaps—and in addition the Tigers should give the Bunnymen two extra shots and the Foxes one extra shot. The Foxes were to give the Rabbits one additional shot.

Cacophonous complaints rent the air, but Jones stood his ground and in the end was entirely vindicated. It was almost a tie for the first time ever. Had the usually steady Tom Steed sunk a short putt at the death, it would have been a tie. But bearded Tom missed handing victory to Terry Chisholm's Foxes by a half a point. The result was Tigers 7.5, Foxes 8.5 and Rabbits 8 points.

But among those bare figures a farcical drama was played out. As the team leaders went out first, Niblick was playing alongside Chisholm and the Tigers' captain Zekia Alsanjak. Both Mashie and Zekia punted their balls to the right on the 7th fairway landing about 10ft apart in two-inch high grass. Zekia reached the balls first and told Niblick that his own ball was slightly to the back of Niblick's. Zek went for the green, but his ball stopped short on the ridge above the green. Niblick hit a pearler, probably his best shot of the day. With the green in a basin—hence its name of the Punch Bowl—he could not see how close to the pin his shot was.

Yet when he got to the ridge above the green on the 265-yard hole, his ball was there. Had his eyes decieved him? They had not. Zekia had played Niblick's ball and Niblick innocently played his opponent's. Not only had his great approach shot been wasted but both players were disqualified for playing the wrong balls. And Niblick's shot with Zekia's ball finished 8ft from the pin, so Mashie had faced the real prospect of a birdie three. It was not to be.

You would have thought that the incident would have prompted the threesome to check their balls properly for the rest of the round. It did not, because it happened again. In yet another farcical encounter, Niblick smashed his ball into gorse bushes near the 16th tee. The ball was easily found, but Niblick had to back into the spiky branches to be able to swing his sand iron. He got the ball out, but then announced: "There you are, I have had free acupuncture in those bushes." He gleefully retailed this news to the Captain's Lady who was then undergoing paid acupuncture treatment from a therapist.

There was time following the afternoon match for Niblick to get home, shower, and amble back to the clubhouse with a decent drinking spell before the formal stag dinner, with the Captain naturally on the top table and parading in his finery. Caterer Gill again provided superb fare and Niblick and one of his mates had the benefit of sharing half of Terry Chisholm's steak pudding as the bulky cabbie was on a special weight-loss diet following major stomach surgery. Then came the presentation of the shield by Mashie Niblick to Chisholm followed by a team photograph. Yet invariably at these presentations, there is alway one idiot missing. So the proud Terry had to show off the shield with only seven of his eight Foxes team members present.

Next it was a proper boozing session with the lads in fine fettle. Niblick could not remember departing the bar, though some claimed that it was gone midnight. Fortunately, one of the lads dropped off Niblick at his house. The skipper went inside, shut the curtains, switched on the television and then awoke at 4am with the TV blaring and the Captain still in his daily togs. In the real bed, he overslept, thus missing the cooked breakfast at the club, and then had one of the most extraordinary confrontations of his entire life.

Niblick was having a final cheese sandwich in his kitchen before heading off to the club to parade around the Sunday lunchtime bar in his Captain's jacket and tie, when a neighbouring house burglar alarm sounded. He thought that he would inspect outside on his way to the club to see whose house alarm was making such a racket. Then the alarm stopped.

Two minutes later, Niblick's telephone rang. It was his neighbour Princess Bulgaria, as the Daily Mail refers to blonde Stella Selwood. She said: "My mobile phone has alerted me to my burglar alarm going off. I am on a boat at Greenwich showing my cousin the sights of London and I cannot get off. Could you investigate? Take your mobile and I'll ring you in five minutes."

Niblick walked the few score yards to her house front, where nothing seemed untoward. But he could not inspect the back of the property because the side gate was locked and bolted. So he walked up to the vestibule and tried the door handle. It let him in. He then tried the main front door handle. It was not locked. Niblick gingerly walked in, past a pair of flip-flops left on the mat, and inspected the downstairs rooms. All seemed in order. His mobile rang. It was Stella. She was flabbergasted when Niblick told her he had got into her home just by opening the doors. "But I locked them before I left," she insisted. "Well if you did, somebody else has unlocked them," replied Niblick.

Stella, who had lost jewellery in a burglary around a year ago, then asked Niblick to go to an upstairs room where she kept what jewellery she had left. Niblick shouted "Anyone in?" as he silently crept up the darkened staircase. There was no reply. But there was a light on in one room.

Niblick went to the door, pushed it open to be confronted by the back of a naked man drying himself after a shower. An intruder who leaves his flip-flops on the mat and then casually has a shower in the princess's bathroom . . . It was absolutely bizarre.

The intruder turned to face Niblick. "What the . . . ?!" said Stella's boyfriend Chris, whom Niblick instantly recognised once he had turned around. "Stella asked me to check out the house after she was notified that the alarm had gone off," explained Niblick. "Here, she's on the other end of my phone. You talk to her."

It transpired that Chris had been out cycling and went into the garage when he got back. This triggered the burglar alarm into screeching. He had thought that Stella was around and was as astonished as Niblick to be confronted in the bathroom.

Anyway, it made a fascinating account when told to members after Niblick finally got to the clubhouse, much later than usual, though some remarked upon his foolhardiness. "You should have dialled 999 and called out the police", remarked one shocked lady member.

The mid-handicap Foxes team whose wiles outdid the clever-clogs Tigers lads and buried the Bunnymen

HOLE 17—HEROIC FAILURE

Mashie Niblick could knock out a longish speech in an hour and a shorter one in 30 minutes. So it was no problem when retired GP Dr Alex Lyons, the seniors' section captain, asked Niblick, as club Captain, to give a short speech before toasting the assembled seniors at their social night. These are the occasions when you can make fun of your fellows and Mashie took full advantage of this, especially as wives and partners were present. This is what he said:

"It seems a little odd for me to be standing here as club Captain about to propose a toast to the seniors' section since I am one of its members. We are a small bunch of golfers but a lively group willing to go out in all sorts of inclement weather as we did in the Seniors' Cup the other week.

"Just like our junior colleagues, we are passionate about the game which has endless fascination in that you can be the dogsbody one week and the prizewinner the next as the handicap system is nominally aimed at sticking all of us on a level playing fairway.

"For, as I remarked at the club's annual dinner-dance recently, golf is a mirror image of life where there are regular ups and downs. But I find that the seniors have many more ups than downs. Take their fixture list: it is peppered with epic outings to local courses where all you pay is the price of lunch. Similarly we enjoy entertaining golfers from other clubs at our jungle course. For all these matches, well over 20 of them, we pay a measly £10 a year for section membership, though this is not quite as big a bargain as it was last year when we just handed over a fiver.

"It is well known—and you golf wives should particularly note this—that golf keeps you fit, adds to your longevity, gets your brain working at full tilt and has a distinctly social dimension as evidenced by this gathering here. It is not, as some detractors maintain, just one remove from the departure lounge; it is indeed the way to keep that particular door firmly shut for decades.

"Golf is a game of character and of characters, which is one of its joys. The other week, I played alongside Duggie Duggan who had his best round of the year finishing runner-up in the John Barnes Cup. I could not have been more delighted at his success as he gets only one golf outing a week since he is the dedicated husband and carer for his lovely wife Margaret and has been for 17 years. (Margaret is wheelchair-bound).

"The more you meet up with other members on the fairways or at the bar of public opinion, the more you realise what a characterful bunch they are. Unless he's just missed a vital putt, there is always a smile on the face of section secretary Peter Rogers or Jolly Rogers as I always think of him.

"Then there's the grim visage of the bearded Tom Steed, the main backwoodsman in the section without a home computer. And the reason for that is that his brain is a computer, famously adept at issuing interpretations of golf's rules.

"While chatting with him at the bar the other week, Hugh Williams, a Welshman and yet another beardie who unfortunately is not here tonight as he has gone to Vienna to pick up a pet rabbit . . . oh and his daughter . . . revealed that he had once worked for six months as a bus conductor before he went to university. Indeed he had to go on a week-long course to learn how to issue tickets. So the next time he wins the Barnes Cup—and he's done it five times already—I shall be delighted to describe him in the local papers as former bus conductor, Cambridge graduate and international stock broker Hugh . . .

"Now this is Captain Alex Lyons' big day of the year. Unless you have been in his position, you will have no idea what problems arise out of the blue on which the Captain has to make a decision, often at short notice and with scant available information. Alex has carried out his duties with aplomb. He has never let down his fellow members and I, for one, salute his dedication to his task and his myriad accomplishments in keeping the section not just afloat, but sailing majestically into 2014. Well done, Alex.

"I could go on and on about the odd traits of our disparate members, but you would be here all night. So I ask you all to raise your glasses as we toast the seniors' section and that is seniors with an 's' apostrophe. Ladies and gentlemen, the Seniors."

The speech went down well. It had that perfect combination of facts and humour, said Niblick, with pointed asides at various members. Most rated it a superb speech of just the right length. "Well," said Niblick, "I might be a passable speech-maker, indeed a selfless promoter of the club, but I'm an abject failure as a golfer which is really the sole attribute that captains need. In truth, I am the Eddie the Eagle of golf." This was a pointed reference to the heroic failure of the English ski-jumper Eddie "the Eagle" Edwards at the Calgary Winter Olympics in Canada in 1988 when he finished a glorious last in two events. Then Mashie put it firmly into context: "Niblick the Navigator", that would be his epitaph if folk ever remembered his golf course indiscretions in the fullness of time.

Just to confirm this, Niblick finished last in the delayed September medal with a worse score than novices who had been playing the game for mere months against Niblick's decades. He did, of course, cite the cases of two notable players who failed to return a card, but two nines and an 11 did for the skipper giving him a lousy 95 nett.

It was the same in the seniors' October medal. He did manage to keep a 10 off his card, though he had three eights and lost only one ball—and that straight into the pond with no possibility of ever retrieving it.

Still, it occurred to Niblick that he was a decided asset to fellow players; the inspiration of playing alongside the captain brought out the best in his partners. In October alone, Brian Meggs had the best round of his life playing with Niblick in the club medal; next Duggie Duggan had his best round of the year alongside Niblick to finish runner-up in the John Barnes Cup; and then Anthony Weaver comfortably won the seniors' October medal when inspired by the Captain's comments on his play. So the message went around: play with Captain Crap if you want to win something . . .

Golf continued in this vein in the last medal of his reign. Alongside novices Neil Robinson and Alan Pickett, Niblick proceeded to dispose of balls like they were bad peaches. While he blamed the balls for being Tory balls, which had a right-swing tendency, and urgently called for more Socialist ones with a left-wing bias, he inwardly knew that it was his pathetic slicing that was the cause. Liberal Democrat balls were not the answer because they were short-length daisy cutters.

In all, eight of Niblick's balls went missing, just about the worst performance—and highest ball loss—of the whole of his golfing year. Inevitably he finished last. This was even when the club had switched from stroke-play to the Captain's favoured stableford points system where all his double figure scores could be conveniently written off as blobs.

And yet his pathetic return of 14 points was hailed by some members as a benchmark for others. Come what may, the Captain always puts in a card, they crowed, unlike some others who were too ashamed to do so or wanted to avoid a handicap cut. Captain Niblick was a true trouper, they claimed. The skipper thought differently. He had not snatched triumph from the jaws of death, but effectively had been eaten.

The Captain's effect came in yet again in the three-club 9-hole event before the seniors' section's annual meeting. Niblick went out with 78-year-old former barber Rob Gibson and naturally, Rob won the competition. Niblick, who used a 2-iron not only as his driver off the tee, but also as his putter, garnered a mere seven points, but was crowing that he lost only one ball. Using his driver as a putter, former Rugby referee Julian Greatrex three-putted almost every hole. Rob, of course, sensibly took out a putter.

It was not all gloom and doom. When the Eclectic table compiled by the moustachioed competitions secretary Michael Jones came out, Niblick had a very respectable 81 gross, admittedly 24 behind postman Mike Everitt, yet a decent enough outcome for all Mashie's forlorn efforts during the year.

In the Eclectic table, your best score for each hole in qualifying competitions is collated by a computer to tell you what would have happened if you had put together a near-perfect round. Niblick equated this to deciding to holiday in Arcadia and play on the Elysian Fields championship course whereby your form was as good as Rory McIlroy in his pomp or Tiger Woods before his marital downfall. It was the stuff of dreams.

Niblick had to admire the ladies' section for they were always looking for ways to boost the income of the club. So that when they fixed up a Cockney Night at the club, he had smartly put his name down for the event and managed to enlist his glamorous neighbour "Princess" Bulgaria and her equally glamorous friend Stanislava to attend in addition to the Captain's Lady. But the general membership was not impressed, even though a goodly number of them could count themselves as expatriate East Enders now basking in the leafy suburbs; the final guest list total was around 30, not really enough to bring in much in the way of funds for the club.

The comedian, the Cockney Sovereign, was a taciturn grey-haired geezer in a black trilby and his session went down well in Niblick's opinion. The Captain's Lady, however, thought he was a misogynist—he definitely was—and too loud, so she shunted off to the ladies' room to read a book. Meanwhile Niblick nodded off, as was his wont at events where he took gallons of beer aboard after a sumptuous dinner.

Heavily slashed membership fees for the tail-end of the year had attracted a trickle of new members, but only a trickle. More needed to be done and the management committee was banking on the new pro, Kenny Banks, having some ideas on this front.

When he and his boss Bradley Preston met members of the management committee, they displayed a positive attitude in suggesting tweaks to the way the club operated. In particular, Kenny asked that members should pop into his shop when about to play so that he could learn who was who and not challenge them for a green-fee token when policing the course, because he did not know who they were and they were not carrying the club 2013 badge on their bags. That seemed a sensible enough idea as was Niblick's that the club might get a buggy so that Kenny could get around the course much faster in his supervisory marshal role and then the buggy could be hired out to members, though a number of ditch bridges would have to be widened if this came about.

What Kenny was now collating was the numbers of players going out on the course at various times and on various days, to get a pattern of usage. The club could, he suggested, have cheaper green fees when there were slack times on slack days. When not being used, the course was a wasted asset. His remarks certainly mirrored Niblick's views.

Once the pros left, there was a heated discussion about the licence the City Corporation wanted the club to sign up to for using their land. While some members, especially the ones who had met up with City officials to discuss the licence, were ready to sign up to it, maverick Stephen Bland, among others, thought that the City was shifting the burden of responsibility on to the club instead of shouldering some of it themselves. The licence was not signed on that night, but it was later on.

77

Niblick's lack of success spilled over from golf to the club's Quiz Night. He reckoned that he had put together a team of magical thinkers and drinkers. They certainly got through more beer than any other table but at a cost; they finished last. And this on the day that the Mansfield Town lads put eight goals past non-league St Albans in the FA Cup away first round, after being a goal down inside eight minutes. What a contrast in fortunes.

Then came the about-turn, which, had it been in a script would have been dismissed as the impossible delusion of a madman: Niblick won something and won it on his own. True it was only the November medal played for by a bunch of seniors. True it was under difficult conditions to start with. And true it was on a day when Niblick despatched only two balls into the undergrowth before declaring them lost.

It happened in a roundabout way and proved to be as big a surprise to fellow competitors as to the Captain himself. There was a hard ground frost, so Niblick chose to use a red ball. After a decent five on the first, he whacked his tee shot, his sixth strike of the day, into the mist on the second, whereupon it took a nasty turn to the left; for once in a while he had found a lefty socialist ball in his bag. But it could not be found. A blob was the outcome, though the sole blob on the Captain's card.

Niblick lost his second ball when he whacked it over the oak trees guarding the short 18th and into thick mounds of grass. He found his provisional, played that out and walked off the course with, according to his partner, John Smith-Pryor, known as JSP, a respectable 32 stableford points. They had been the first group out on the frosty fairways, but finished the game in glorious sunshine.

But once Tom Steed, the veteran competition secretary, checked the card, he found that Niblick had been done out of two points, thus giving him 34 points against his partner's 33. This still did not register in Niblick's brain so used was he to being tail-end Mashie. Indeed, JSP apologised claiming he misread the Captain's handicap as 25 when it was actually 28.

Niblick protested when "Aussie" Ray Jones, the expatriate Queenslander, was awarded the best-front-nine bottle of wine with 16 points when JSP had garnered 18 points. Even when told that you cannot win two prizes in a medal, Mashie still inhabited a nightmare world of defeat after reverse.

It was when JSP was called up to accept the runner-up prize that it finally dawned on the Captain that he must be the winner. And so it came about. On his first outing as the new captain of the seniors' section, John Walker insisted on having a photograph taken of himself handing the glass trophy to Niblick because this was an image for posterity should anyone be daft enough to write a history of the club since its 1990 centenary.

The trophy took pride of place on Niblick's lounge mantelpiece because it was the only trophy he had ever won by individual play; previously he had held on to the coat-tails of others to get his name in lights.

With not only the days shortening after the clocks were turned back, the end of the reign of the Captain was now in sight. So Niblick, having been chivvied by his former sidekick Terry Insole, decided that as he had come into the captaincy with a bang having performed the Outlaw sketch before his drive-in, he would now go out with a bang in holding a farewell party he labelled the LAST HURRAH.

Once he had fixed on the date, a Sunday four days before he became remaindered as one of a host of past captains, he took up barmaid Emma Dorrington's suggestion for hiring Andy, the Hertfordshire disc jockey Emma had used for her wedding earlier in the year, and then arranged for caterer Gill Templeman to provide a two-course lunch for £12 a head with the main dish being Niblick's favourite steak pie.

Niblick then stuck up posters advertising the event where he would ride in to the club's lounge on Woody, his prized hobby horse, before giving a rousing rendition of "Slagheaps of my Youth" while still mounted and being accompanied by the Captain's Lady as the fiddler on the hoof. It was yet another ruse by what some saw as a crackpot captain. If nothing else, said Niblick, 2013 would go down as one of the most memorable years in the 123-year history of the club, not just because of what happened but the fact that his amenuensis had recorded it from start to finish. What other skipper among the 4,000 golf clubs in Britain could boast that? said Mashie.

Captain Niblick as seen by greenkeeper Stuart Runciman, an artist of the greensward

This was the denoument; the time when the members of the club learned of the tome compiled from the moment Niblick was asked to be captain until the late November day in 2013 when he shed his authority in favour of the 2014 captain, Zekia Alsanjak.

Only the Captain's Lady had known of this writing venture for more than a year, although Mashie Niblick had to reveal the plot when he contacted various literary agents. As you would expect with Niblick's luck, every single agent rebuffed him as they had in the past snubbed J.K.Rowling and, for that matter, The Beatles. So he took the modern route to publishing glory—the internet.

After handing Zekia the Captain's green jacket at the club's annual meeting in a scene reminiscent of the Masters anointing of the Augusta National winner in Georgia, Niblick waited until Any Other Business before making his announcement. It was greeted with laughter partly because of the way Niblick delivered it with pauses and emphases and partly because of the choice of name of the imposter. Apart from a few folk who said that they would definitely buy it, it made only a modest impression on the membership, apart from Mark Bonham who demanded the first signed copy.

Mashie Niblick's sole aim was to promote the golf club, to let the world know what a magic gem lay hidden in Epping Forest in north-east London. If he succeeded in that then he was happy. He wanted the 125th anniversary of the club's formation in 2015 to be marked by a huge increase in its membership and the club being able to shed its previous hand-to-mouth existence. If that happened, getting his amanuensis to write an account of his soaring showman's talent and his pathetic golfing regress had been worthwhile.

Niblick's steed Woody neighs into the microphone as the Captain's Lady looks on at the Last Hurrah party

How had Niblick himself fared during his Captain's year? It was a mixed potage. Undoubtedly in golfing terms, he was the dodgiest player to be captain in living memory. Most club captains can perform on the course and they tend to have a decent playing pedigree. True Niblick too had a pedigree, but it was not one most golfers would care to boast about. He styled himself the world's worst golf captain and could garner enough evidence on that score to fill a large golf bag.

During his captaincy, his handicap went up to the maximum accorded to novices. He could not even break 100 during his reign. His successes came largely on the coat-tails of others. He had never ever won any cup or trophy or even a humdrum medal individually on his own account right up until his dying days when the prospect of soon being remaindered loomed.

And yet he had enjoyed his reign. Being greeted as "Captain" by his men—and a goodly number of women—chuffed him up considerably; always being on the top table and getting his food served first was what he reckoned he deserved in life; regularly getting his picture in local papers boosted his ego; while parading around the bar on Sunday lunchtimes in his fancy jacket and tie was what he had been born to do. He was a natural at this bar of public opinion and an unnatural on the tee, the fairway and the green.

He started his year as a confirmed trolley puller and while his brother, the Professor, still a bag carrier aged 71, derided him for that, Niblick himself looked down loftily upon those many members with electric trolleys as southern softies.

That was until Niblick himself purchased cheaply a second-hand electric trolley and, like a revelation on the fairway to Damascus GC, he overnight became a confirmed electric trolley wally.

Niblick's consumption of alcohol, always high in Fleet Street watering holes for more than 30 years, actually diminished a tiny bit. But that was only because the Captain had developed a tendency to nod off after several pints of bitter. Had he been as capable of staying awake as he was in his prime, bar profits at the club, already high, would have been even higher.

Captains come and captains go. Some are leaders, others are led. There are as many types of captain as there are termites in a tower house built of bunker sand. Niblick reckoned that he could count himself one of the fortunate ones, remembered not for any achievements or accomplishments or for playing disasters, but for just being himself, unvarnished and understated.

That became evident when he funded a Last Hurrah party at the clubhouse four days before he became just one more gold name on the historic Captains board. Scores attended, coughing up a fiver each for the Captain's Charity—the golf club—and the Captain felt humbled when the lads laughingly presented him with a golf game to be played while perched on the lavatory seat as well as a small ball marker with a stag's head on it and the legend "Mansfield Town Football Club".

This came after Niblick had ridden into the clubhouse on his trusty steed, Woody the hobby horse, to more blasts from his hunting horn and yet another rendition of "Slagheaps of my Youth" with a violin serenade from the Captain's Lady, the fiddler on the hoof, in between verses.

Was it worth it? Of course, opined Niblick. True, he had neglected his garden and its plants, he had just about abandoned thoughts of creating more artworks while in office, had severely cut back on his gallery-going and oft times failed to read the immense numbers of sections produced by the Telegraph at weekends.

What had he achieved during his year? Precious little. In truth, his sole achievement was to arrange for the buying of a promotional banner, yet this flag had spent almost as much time being repaired as fluttering in the forecourt breeze and it was still undergoing repair on the day that he stepped down. All those epic speeches to the management committee turned out to be waffle, high-falutin' waffle, but waffle all the same.

Yet the compensations more than made up for this: there are few things finer, he asserted, than driving off into the greensward on a fairway lined with trees and the sun beating down on your back and believing that the world is a magical place which has reinvented itself just for you and your companions on this pristine day.

You feel like shouting: "It's great to be alive" because it is, whether you win or whether you sin. And so, instead of signing all his correspondence "Ye Captain" in his inimitable way, the adventure came to an end on November 21, 2013, when Niblick was remaindered. Sad but inevitable. You only live once and by and large, you only become captain once, the skipper opined.

Of course, the lads managed to take the mickey out of the Captain after a few folk praised his efforts in the role at the annual meeting. Then up strode 2003 Captain Tom Steed to tell of his horror at playing with Niblick clad in cycle clips to stop his trousers getting wet when the pair of them won the Seniors' Shield. So Tom presented the past skipper with a pair of luminous trouser straps.

Niblick said that as there was a ban on golfers rolling up their trousers and sticking them inside their socks, he knew there was no prohibition on wearing cycle clips, which was why he had craftily defeated the rules. Instantly, journalist Jill James proposed a ban on cycle clips. She received no support. Another triumph for Niblick.

HOLE 19—IMPOSTER

Quite a number of readers will have twigged early on that the un-named golf club is at Sunset Avenue, Woodford Green on the outskirts of north-east London. The reason it was just referred to as "the club" was simply because the author wished the account not to be about a specific club, but about any club anywhere.

Additionally, he did not want to present himself as the dodgy captain never ever able to win a competition on his own ability, but hanging on the coat sleeves of more competent players, as he undoubtedly was. Thus he invented Mashie Niblick as his alter ego. In this way he could record the true events of the day, but slightly distance himself from them as though they were happening not to the real skipper but to the imaginary Captain Niblick.

Now in creating this pseudonym, the author chose the names of two old-style irons. The mashie was roughly a 7 iron and a niblick an 8 iron in today's parlance. These names were used 100 years ago when golf was a game for the privileged. Then golf professionals were course designers and club makers. They made individual clubs for particular golfers, to their height and build. So that a niblick made in Dundee for a slim banker could be very different from the niblick made for a portly Nottingham lawyer.

With the mass production of golf clubs, standardisation became the norm and irons were given numbers. Even 50 years ago in the woods compartment of golf bags, there were still the driver, the brassie (No 2 wood) and the spoon (No 3 wood) as well as the baffy (no 4 wood). Apart from the driver, all the other wood names have bitten the dust as club manufacturers ditched persimmon to concentrate on the loft of fairway "woods" now made of metal and no longer with wooden shafts.

So in creating Captain Mashie Niblick, the author has relied on ancient club terminology. The author's golfing life stretches over 60 years, so that he has a perspective, moving from caddy to captain, that younger golfers do not possess. It was the author's intention to pass on some of this golfing history to a new generation of players vastly superior in their course skills to the folk he played with decades ago in England and in Africa.

Golf is now more popular than it ever has been and there are millions who have taken up the cudgels once they realised that the handicap system ostensibly makes golf a level playing field for both old hands and young Turks. It keeps you fit, it keeps you healthy, it fosters the competitive spirit and it provides a vibrant social life. What more could you want?

Now that you are aware that Captain Mashie Niblick is an imposter, it is incumbent upon the author to thank the officials and members of Woodford Golf Club for their forbearance. Until he announced that he had written this account of the travails of a club captain after he handed over the captaincy to the man who wrote the words to the Turkish-Cyriot national anthem, one Zekia Alsanjak, at the annual meeting, not one soul in the club knew that the author was clandestinely penning this account. Only the Captain's Lady knew of his devious plan, as the author maintained that this subterfuge was the only way to get a genuine and true version of life at the blade face. If golfers had known about his daily jottings, they would have changed their behaviour. It is the old social science story of how waiters act differently among their peers in the kitchen compared to how they perform obsequiously when dealing face-to-face with restaurant diners.

This is a true account of a captain's year, but a particular captain with an upbringing and life experience different from every one of the 4,000 other captains elected annually at clubs across Great Britain. And yet most of them face familiar problems which surface as regularly as clocks moving forward or back in spring and autumn—subscription fees, dress codes and course design changes to name but a few.

They always will. Life does not ossify. Life is change. The clubs the author first used are antediluvian; museum pieces even. Technology is constantly improving the performance of the clubs we use and will continue to do so. The burning question is how we utilise these undoubted benefits because in the end it is golfers' skills that are paramount. Significantly, championship courses are being lengthened and reshaped to cope with the long hitters and their fancier flying balls. We will never reach that Elysian Fields course where pars are the norm for modest players, except in our dreams, thank goodness.

*   *   *

Now the author, in his other guise as Captain Robin Hood, launched his year with an Outlaw sketch, the like of which had never before been seen on the greensward of Woodford golf course. This is how it played on November 18, 2012:

OUTLAW SKETCH performed by the Red Army ensemble

SCENE: the edge of Epping Forest, north-east London

(Robin Hood, riding a hobby horse and furiously blowing his hunting horn, leads the Outlaws singing the Robin Hood theme tune on to the greensward labelled 10th tee; Alan A'Dale strums his ukelele and jester George A'Green does a jig)

Hood: Friends, Woodsmen and countrymen, my Merry Marxists have decamped from Sherwood after hearing that London is a deer place. We have come to check out the game.

Much the Miller's son: Oh dear, oh dear, oh dear.

Hood: We are 21st century forest outlaws. We track the Sheriff by GPS satellite and we communicate via smartphones.

(The Merry Men all pull mobile phones out of their pockets and begin dialling. As they do so, club secretary Peter Willett nips across the tee and whispers into Robin's ear)

Hood: Forsooth. Lads we're stuffed. Phones banned on the golf course and no deer have been seen in the last two years. We will have to hunt golf balls.

David of Doncaster: Before a-hunting we will go, Commissar, what will we do with Cheryl of Nottingham, the sheriff's daughter whom we kidnapped in Mansfield yesterday?

(In the background stands the forlorn and tearful Cheryl in handcuffs; the men turn to point at her)

Hood: Well, what should we do with her my merry Marxmen?

Chorus: Hang her.

Alan A'Dale: String her up from the tallest oak in the woods.

Cheryl of Nottingham: Help! help!

George A'Green: Diddly dum. Diddly dum. Diddly dee.

Friar Tuck: My lord have mercy on this terrified lass, Amen, Awomen, Apersons.

Hood: OK priestly one. I shall show the compassion that her wicked father never does.

(Hood waves his arms in the air)

Hood: Maid Marian and Mistress Karen, march this petrified virgin off to our camp. I want her behind bars serving foaming pints of honest English ale to my men when we return from the hunt.

(Little John bangs his staff on the ground)

Little John: But Comrade Sire . . .

(Hood dismissively waves him away)

Hood (shouting): Marian, Karen, don't let the lothario Little John within 10 paces of this manacled wench.

Maid Marian and Mistress Karen: Aye, aye, master.

(Hood turns to Scarlett)

Hood: Now then Will, get out your iPad and email the Sheriff demanding a ransom of 100 florins for his daughter. Stick it on Facebook as well.

Scarlett (incredulous): ONE HUNDRED florins?

Hood: Yes, I plan to buy the Tower of London and with the change the infamous Hyde Park, haunt of toffs and tarts. Let's show that we mean business. Bring me your bows of burning gold, bring me your arrows of desire . . .

(The Merry Men line up with their toy bows and load their rubber sucker-tipped arrows)

Hood: Fore!

(A fusillade of arrows plop on the tee; Robin and the Merrie Men bow to the assembled golfers. There then follows the actual drive-in.)

CAST: Robin Hood (Captain Mashie Niblick); Friar Tuck (Martin Cox); Will Scarlett (Colin Thompson); Maid Marian (Susanna Ferrar); Alan A'Dale (Terry Insole); Mistress Karen, Lady of the Bedchamber (Karen Verney); Little John (John Beecroft); Much the Miller's son (Kevin Sullivan); George A'Green, the forest jester (Vincent Thompson); David of Doncaster (Steve Parker); Cheryl of Nottingham (Cheryl Cook); Hobo, the Sherwood ruffian (Dave Rowell); with grateful assistance from club secretary Peter Willett. Script and direction by Capt Niblick.

Before the one-off performance came the business of preparing the costumes. The Captain's Lady offered to make green tabards for the Merry Men, while Niblick ordered a Friar Tuck tonsure for big Martin Cox and a costume for himself plus seven sets of toy bows and arrows as he feared getting proper bows would upset the health and safety mafia. Authenticity was not an issue. The wandering minstrel Alan A'Dale would have to make do with a ukelele rather than a medieval stringed instrument while the forest comic, George A'Green, was quite capable of making a fool of himself even without a daft jester's cap, all violent colours and jingling bells.

After all, said Niblick, all history is bunk, according to one prominent and long-departed American. This Hood business may have an element of truth in it, it may not. "It's a brilliant legend and we'll exploit it as we wish just like film companies over the years".

This Hood, said the captain, he invented communism centuries before Karl Marx was even born and it was vastly more successful in Sherwood than any of the ludicrous 19th century poetic pantisocrasies that failed time after time. They are still with us though, these pantisocracies usually in the form of religious sects headed by a charismatic lunatic desperate for sexual congress with as many women as he can lure to his den.

The captain's green jacket of office with its club badge and inscription "Captain 2013" was successfully put together at the back street tailor in Forest Gate and subsequently checked out for size before being collected by Niblick. And this genial tailor, "Steve" Stephens, tipped off "Maid Marian" where to find relatively cheap cloth for the tabards at a shop opposite Upton Park station as well as women's wear from the nearby Queen's market.

Little by little the gear ordered off the internet—the Friar Tuck outfit, the jester's hat and Woody, the braying hobby horse, and such like—turned up at the Niblick abode and 10 days before the performance, Niblick ordered a read-through rehearsal so that the lads and lasses, even though they had only a few words to say, would know just where in the sketch they had to speak out. Yet it was a shambolic affair.

This was especially the case when Niblick read out the line describing Cheryl of Nottingham as a petrified virgin. "Some virgin," cried out her partner. "She's got three kids." This left the bar mob writhing with laughter and poor Niblick aghast as he was already short of both Friar Tuck and David of Doncaster on the night and trying valiantly to play their parts as well as his own.

On a run-through in his own home, Niblick had timed the sketch at 2 minutes, 57 seconds. Barman Adam reckoned this slapdash reading took five minutes even allowing for the numerous interruptions.

This was hopeless, Niblick told himself. There was another read-through, though not really much better. The whole point of a snappy sketch was to attempt to get the local TV news programmes to broadcast it on a slack-news Sunday. Niblick had already emailed the newsdesks of three broadcasters, but only provoked a smidgeon of interest from the BBC, who failed to follow up an initial inquiry.

As a former Fleet Street newsdesk operative himself—once glorying in the title of Chief Assistant News Editor—Niblick well knew the failings of some of these politically-obsessed petty mandarins who would not recognise a popular story if it bit them on the arse. Facebook would show them all up, he said to himself.

In a bid to propel the club from semi-obscurity to regional prominence, Niblick had already enlisted support from two local papers, one of which quite blatantly used one of Niblick's own reports word for word and slapped the byline of "Kirk Blows" on it. Unfazed, Niblick sent messages to the newsdesks of the Daily Telegraph, The Times, Independent, Daily Mail and Evening Standard alerting them to the jolly sketch club members were to perform. He thought that the Standard might swallow the bait, maybe none of the others, but they could never attend if they were not told that it would be happening. Not one bit the the cherry.

Later on in the evening, one young club member confessed to having never heard Niblick's epic poem the "Slagheaps of my Youth". The author proposed giving him an instant rendition. Boos and catcalls led all the members to march out of the clubhouse making plain that they had heard it once a fortnight for a year and would not endure it again. Niblick's face really was plastered in dung when the young lad joined the reprobates.

The dress rehearsal 35 hours afore the actual performance went pretty well, even though the loose cannon David of Doncaster failed to show up as did Alan A'Dale and Cheryl of Nottingham. New member Anna Maris read these parts quite niftily until the bar fell apart when George A'Green in his daft jester's hat and gumboots did a mock sign-language spoof behind Niblick in his Robin Hood garb. Niblick ordered a single malt whisky to recover.

Dave Rowell, a notorious exhibitionist—he regularly volunteers to wear the thong of shame on the beach at Torremolinos—arrived and demanded to be in the sketch despite the fact that he had turned down the important role of Friar Tuck early on because he claimed he was not fat enough. So Niblick, ever the compassionate colleague, gave him the role of Hobo, the Sherwood ruffian, a peasant never before reported in the annals of legend versions down the centuries. Dave wanted Sue Ferrar, the Captain's Lady, to run him up a tabard sewn down both sides as he planned to appear in fishnet tights and did not want to expose his suspenders to an astonished world. The Captain's Lady gamely worked on this from 11pm until 1am of the morning of the sketch only for Dave to hitch his special costume up to his waist anyway, displaying the suspenders it had been designed to cover.

As he had fully expected, the bow and arrows sets ordered from the gormless RedSave internet toyshop never arrived and in desperation, Niblick telephoned Debs Shrimpton of the local archery club to see if he could borrow a longbow. He could not because of all sorts of safety reasons, but Debs did offer a flicker of hope in suggesting that Niblick should contact Perris Archery, a store that might be able to help if I asked for jelly bows and bobcats. It would mean a Saturday drive into Essex to collect them if all else failed.

Penny Northcott, Niblick's younger daughter, saved the captain's bacon. He was moaning about the lack of medieval weapons to his daughter, who said that she was just about to go shopping in Canterbury and would look out for these toys. An hour later she telephoned Niblick to announce that she had got seven plastic bows and arrows from a shop at £2.50 each—a lot cheaper than the RedSave firm was charging. Manna from a medieval heaven.

It prompted Niblick to send a jaunty message of cheer to the valiant thespians of the Red Army ensemble, so called because a significant item of red clothing has to be worn by players on the golf course. It read:

FOR ONE MORNING ONLY

Despite the failure of David of Doncaster, Alan A'Dale, and Cheryl of Nottingham to attend the dress rehearsal of the Outlaw sketch at the club last night, the Red Army ensemble is shipshape, Mansfield fashion as the first run-through was fine. The really good news is that we now have seven sets of toy plastic bows and arrows purchased this very morning by my daughter Penny in Canterbury. The internet firm that has badly let me down is called RedSave. Incidentally, I have now found the brown cassock for Friar Tuck and will bring it to the club early tomorrow morning. The Sherwood Ruffian (alias Dave Rowell) will have his sewn-down-the-sides tabard made tonight by Maid Marian once she returns from a foray into Norfolk, but sadly she cannot provide this exhibitionist camp follower with fishnet stockings.

I thought the outfits put together by jester George A'Green and Much the Miller's son last night, as well as the medieval garb to be worn by ye Maid Marian (as well as Mistress Karen, though I have not yet seen her in all her pomp) are absolutely stunning. All I need now is the pair of handcuffs to be provided by Guy Wade and we are all set to stupefy the club golfers with a magnificent display of Performance Art.

As regards tomorrow, I shall ask all bacon-butty and malt-whisky golfers except the Red Army ensemble to vacate the changing rooms by 8.30am, giving us around five minutes to don our costumes and be ready to prance out to the 10th tee to the sound of blasts from my hunting horn and singing by the Merry Men. The sketch will last 3-4 minutes and ends after Robin the Hoodie shouts "Fore" and the Merry archers fire their arrows. Then the ensemble bows to the audience and we prepare for the real business of the day, the Captain's drive-in. After that, we need to disrobe and wear our normal red golfing gear for the Texas Scramble competition. Gill is providing lunch for those of us who have put our names down on her list. Music will be played by Jingles from 3-7pm. A good time will be had by all—and that's the Captain's order of the day.

May I give all of the Red Army ensemble (plus Anna Maris, the prompt, and Paul Verney, the photographer) my grateful thanks for their participation in this comedy sketch and not just participation but wholesale espousal of its Monty Pythonesque humour in launching a fantastic start to the Captain's year. You are a magnificent lot. You all will make this Captain's year, a proper year to remember . . .

I am, sirs and ladies, your humble servant

Captain Robin Hood

*   *   *

Niblick carefully prepared his bombshell speech to the membership given during Any Other Business at the close of the annual meeting. Now as Past Captain, this is how he launched his missile:

"A year ago on accepting the club captaincy, I said that we all needed to create a special magic here to rebuild the membership of the club. Every week since then, I have diligently—and clandestinely—been pursuing this single aim.

"When first approached by Mark Bonham to be his surprise vice-captain, I decided on a course of action which is just coming to fruition. I looked around the 4,000 or so golf clubs in Britain, each with their own captains, men of talent, men of intellect and men of the people. Over a span of 10 years, that would mean that 40,000 golfers would have been elected by their peers to the role. And yet, so far as I can ascertain, not one of them has written an account of the life of an ordinary golf club captain.

"Ladies and gentlemen, I have rectified that. I have penned an account of life at the coalface, so to speak, to alert sportsmen and women at large to the glories of this small club. It has been written by me, but using an alter ego. Thus Captain Mashie Niblick is the hero and the villain of this true story. This man standing before you is merely his amenuensis. I find it much easier to distance myself from what is happening in this real golfing life and attribute the unfolding events to Niblick, at times a buffoon, at times a loudmouth, at times a cleverdick, at oft times a boozer, but always a lousy golfer.

"Perhaps that is the secret. Who really wants to hear more boastful accounts of birdies and eagles shot by millionaire professionals? Their books are ten a penny, invariably penned by ghost writers. Captain Niblick is the genuine article, the humdrum man of the people, a toper, a showman, an eccentric. He tells it how it really is, whether thrashing about in the jungle beneath our forest of trees or donning the thong of shame on the beach at Torremolinos. And if you want to blame anyone for Niblick's invention, look towards Mark Bonham. Had he not made the crackpot decision to ask me to be his Deputy Dawg, Mashie Niblick would never have been born.

"Though I say it myself, the Captain Niblick book is shot through with humour. It does not mention Woodford until the 19th hole, with each chapter being labelled a hole. The idea was not to be specific as to the name of the actual club, but to consider it as Everyclub. Nevertheless, just about all that happens in the book happened right here.

"I have not been in this for self-aggrandisment, merely to broadcast the benefits of club membership. Profits from the book will be shared between the golf club and me. "Captain Niblick—the world's worst golf skipper" which is its title, will first appear as a book to download from the internet, later as a paperback. At present it is a base metal which can be transformed into an element of value. Its success or failure will rest upon you. If you like it and persuade friends and relatives of its intrinsic worth as well as promoting it on social network sites, then Woodford Golf Club will be on to a winner.

"We will, I would dare to suggest, be the envy not just of other clubs in the Essex Golf Union, but across the nation. Ladies and gentlemen, a fair number of you folk will have unknowingly been featured in its pages because I have deliberately kept quiet about its compilation. Only the Captain's Lady has been aware of my jottings. The reason that I wanted to keep it secret was so that it would be an authentic account of a captain's year-long tenure and there would be no-one playing to the gallery. That much said, it is an account filtered through my eyes; others experiencing the same events might well have a different perspective.

"So, ladies and gentlemen, I end my captaincy on a similar high to the day it was launched with the merry Outlaw sketch. Let us all hope that the sound of Captain Niblick's hunting horn is a portent of more prosperous times for the club and all its members.

"Thank you".

ACKNOWLEDGEMENTS

Whether they feature by name or not in the book, the author salutes all the members and staff of Woodford Golf Club for making 2013 such a memorable year.

It may seem invidious to single out particular people, but I have full-heartedly to praise drinking pal Major Terry Insole, the 2004 skipper and my one-time sidekick for his constant support and ideas, quite a few of which the Captain took up. In my time at the club, he has been its finest captain and also a magnificent recruiting sergeant.

Then there is Peter Willett, the club Secretary, who was always on hand to proffer advice and to tell the Captain when he needed to provide yet more port for the delectation of members.

The Captain's Lady, Susanna Ferrar, kept quiet about this whole writing project from its inception and garnished the later renditions of "Slagheaps" by supplying a violin accompaniment. Not the least of her talents is as proof-reader to ensure that the Captain's words are as he intended them.

Members of the Friday «whip mob» who were on hand every week to take the Captain down a peg or two or three.

Young Mark Bonham (well, young compared to the Captain's advanced age) for having the crackpot notion that I would make a passable skipper, because without that invitation, Captain Mashie Niblick would never have been born.

The greenkeeper and caricaturist Stuart Runciman - an artist of the greensward - for supplying a natty image of the skipper as Robin Hood, beer paunch and all.

All those folk who took magical pictures and films of the Outlaw sketch and other events, among them Anna Maris, Lynne Wade, Paul Verney, Nicholas Wade, Sean Marah, Christine Wade and Penny Northcott, although the Captain himself later on took a goodly few.

Zekia Alsanjak for taking up the cudgels as vice-captain when I approached him to be my dogsbody.

Outside the confines of the golfing community, there was David Green who turned my idea of a book cover close to reality by cleverly photographing golf implements so that his pal John Maclean, could merge them plus text into a stunning cover.

And not forgetting my publishers, Xlibiris, who speeded up the turn-round of my words into an electronic book and then a physical entity. Their assistance was invaluable.

Captain Mashie Niblick's thoughts for the days. Some of the wisdom and wit of the Captain as distilled by his amanuensis either in the book, on the course, or at the bar of public opinion:

* The Captain's word is law.

* Membership is the lifeblood of any club, be it golf or tiddlywinks.

* Venerate women for they are our past, our present and our future.

* A peripatetic player merely enjoys a platonic relationship with any course or club; a member has that much deeper commitment, almost akin to marriage.

* Always shower or bathe before a consultation with a medical professional.

* If you cheat at golf, you undermine your own self-respect.

* Beware the blandishments of the "John Daley breakfast" deal to lure you to a distant golf course.

* "That was bullshit" - the Captain's riposte to an innocent remark.

* "That was absolute bullshit" - the Captain's comment on a barbed criticism of his views.

* "The world is full of bullshit" - the essence of the Captain's ideology.

* Don't whinge and whine when you lose a golf ball in dense undergrowth; you're still alive unlike my bosom mate Gary Marney, who dropped dead at 52 in 2010. What would he give to be in your shoes...?

* Golfing itinerants never ever get their names in gold letters on honours boards.

* Rely on your own eyes, not on satellite navigation or fairway yardage scopes.

* Play golf and live longer.

* Play golf in Shakespeare country and suffer the slings and arrows of outrageous fortune.

* The fairway is the perfect name for a route to happiness or despair.

* Anyone who names a work of art "Untitled" displays an appalling lack of verbal dexterity.

* "Beer not bubbles" - the Captain's riposte to bar staff offering short-measure pints.

* Honest English real ale, the nectar of the gods.

* Single malt Scottish whisky, the ultimate tipple of Bacchus, the Greek god of alcohol.

* Buy a daily newspaper for these organs are the backbone of our civilisation, something that Facebook and

Twitter can never aspire to.

* Real relationships are forged in clubs and bars or at work, not on social network sites.

* Be pleasant and cheery to folk and they will repay you a hundredfold.

* Unless you are a blatant exhibitionist, take out insurance against being obliged to wear the mankini on a Torremolinos beach.

* Sinking a long putt gives a fillip not far short of a sexual climax and especially once you have been allocated a pensioner's bus pass.

* The nearest Niblick normally gets to a birdie is spotting a green woodpecker among the legion of magpies on the course.

* Keep a daily diary then you can look back with astonishment on your past achievements and current ordinariness.

* Always heartily toast a winner for it may be your turn to receive the plaudits in some future competition.

* No matter how dire, always post your competition score for thereby you will gain the reputation of being Honest John.

* Greet passers-by with a "Good Morning" salutation and you will enhance their cheerfulness.

* For every winner, there are 20, 200 or 20,000 losers depending on the sport.

* Do not despair for there is always tomorrow.

* Golf lessons from professionals ultimately pay dividends.

* Beware the blandishments of the greenkeeper's nubile daughter.

* If the driving power of your youth has dissipated, then follow the Bill Deedes fair way of punting the ball in a straight line 100 yards at a time and you will be on most greens in four strokes or fewer.

* Deadly putting is the key to low scores.

* Golf is like life: the more you put into it, the more you get out of it.

* Confidence is the key to a happy life and decent golfing prowess.

* Dress appropriately for the occasion. If you wear a tramp's garb, people will treat you as a tramp; wear toffs' clothes and folk will treat you like a toff.....that is until you open your mouth.

* Stick to your last for practising does work.

* My best ideas come as I lie awake in bed. So keep a notebook and pencil on the bedside table.

* By replacing divots, you not only keep the course in fine fettle, you rob thieving magpies of easy worm pickings.

* Unless you are Lee Westwood, just remember that a brand-new driver which will give you another 10 yards off the tee will also put you 10 yards further into the rough. (Incidentally, Niblick was playing with his own Dad at Worksop golf course before Lee was born in Worksop).

* Don't forget that the young lad caddying for you could be the next Tiger Woods or even, forsooth, the next Captain Niblick.

* Ensure that your golf shoes do not leak, your trousers and casual top are rainproof, that you carry a brolly and then you are equipped for summer golf in Britain.

* Walk everywhere you can when it is feasible to stop your brain from shrinking.

* One for the strasse" is always one more than you need.

* While he is in office, the Captain is the fount of all knowledge.

* A polymath is a Captain in disguise.

* Fame is as fleeting as a February of 30 days.

* If you don't want thieves to steal your car, drive a reliable battered banger.

* Never leave the house while the dishwasher or clothes washer are running.

* If golf was easy, nobody would bother with it.

* Whenever faced with a challenge, go for it.

* Always cultivate younger folk as friends then you will have a decent bevy of mourners at your funeral.

* Sign in the captain's downstairs toilet with lines of type in diminishing sizes: IF SIR, you cannot read the last line of this notice, then Sir, you are not standing close enough to the lavatory bowl.

* Cometh the hour, cometh the maniac.

* A hole in one is golfing nirvana.

* The aura that surrounds a Captain does not mean that he is invincible, merely notable.

* Every self-respecting Captain should ensure that he plays at least one round of golf in Scotland, the cradle of the game, during his term of office.

* Chance rules all our lives.

* A spinster in want of a husband should join a golf club - with apologies to Jane Austen.

* For a prosperous future back the Stock Market rather than Newmarket.

* Dog walkers should note that a golf course is a missile firing range.

* It is people who make life such a breeze.

* Remember the three easy "Es" of golf: enjoyment, exercise and etiquette.

* Power without responsibility - the prerogative of the post-menopausal widow.

* Amateur players with huge golf bags usually have egos to match them.

* Mishaps generally come in threes.

* Beware of chorizo baguettes sold at Spanish airports.

* Golfers are even bigger liars than anglers.

* A golf club without a professional is akin to a headless chicken.

* The biggest yobs you find invading golf courses en masse are immature schoolboys.

* Confidence is the key to life, the universe and golf.

* A missed putt is not the end of the world, only the end of the hole.

* Wafflers gravitate to golf club committees.

* Keeping a proper daily diary galvanizes the brain to combat senility.

* Maintain your focus, especially while putting.

* Join a golf club to make new friends and boost your social life.

* If you want free acupuncture, just whack you ball into a clump of gorse bushes.

* Immerse yourself totally in a subject to become an expert.

* Quiz Night teams are made up of thinkers and drinkers.